THE PARADOXES OF DEMOCRACY

Kermit Eby and June Greenlief

A HADDAM HOUSE BOOK

The Paradoxes
of Democracy

Association Press, New York

THE PARADOXES OF DEMOCRACY

Copyright © 1956 by
National Board of Young Men's Christian Associations

Association Press, 291 Broadway, New York 7, N. Y.

Library of Congress catalog card number: 56-6452

 2

Printed in the United States of America

Contents

Chapter 1

The one common calling is that of citizenship. The one common destiny is that of manhood.

—ROBERT MAYNARD HUTCHINS

The Common Destiny

ASSUMING that "the one common destiny is that of manhood," what are the problems that face the average citizen in a democracy which claims liberty and freedom as its cornerstones?

The question I would raise concerns why we prefer democratic and humane arrangements to those which are autocratic and harsh. And by "why" I mean the *reason* for preferring them, not just the *causes* which lead us to the preference. One *cause* may be that we have been taught not only in the schools but by the press, the pulpit, the platform, and our laws and law-making bodies that democracy is the best of all social institutions. We may have so assimilated this idea from our surroundings that it has become an habitual part of our mental and moral make-up. But similar causes have led other persons in different surroundings to widely varying conclusions—to prefer fascism, for example. The cause for our preference is not the same thing as the reason why we *should* prefer it.

It is not my purpose here to go in detail into the reason. But I would ask a single question: Can we find any reason that does not ultimately come down to the belief that democratic social arrangements promote a better quality of human experience, one which is widely accessible and enjoyed, than do nondemocratic and antidemocratic forms of social life? . . . Is it not the reason for our preference that we believe that mutual consultation and convictions, reached through persuasion, make possible a better quality of experience than can otherwise be provided on any wide scale?[1]*

—JOHN DEWEY

How can man develop his individuality without being considered "queer" in a society which imposes its desires through public opinion? How is he free to say or to do what he wishes when his government, which he believes has given him that freedom, is so baffling in its hugeness and complexity that it inevitably forces him to accept its decisions? How has the spirit of the geographical frontier left its imprint on the American man's attitudes and aims today? Why must there be, along with the recognition of freedom, a recognition of difference in this heterogeneous society of ours? Is the common man making his greatest mistake in failing to understand that living the good life is always and everywhere the most important goal toward which all men can strive? These are some of the questions with which this chapter deals.

Mass Man Versus the Individual

"The characteristic of the hour," cries Ortega y Gasset, "is that the commonplace mind, knowing itself to be

* All footnotes are given by chapters at the end of the book.

commonplace, has the assurance to proclaim the rights
of the commonplace and to impose them wherever it
will. As they say in the United States: 'to be different is
to be indecent.' . . . The old democracy was tempered
by a generous dose of liberalism and of enthusiasm for
law. . . . Today we are witnessing the triumphs of a
hyperdemocracy in which the mass acts directly, outside
the law, imposing its aspirations and its desires by means
of material pressures. . . . That is why I speak of *hyperdemocracy*."[2]

With this initial generalization, Ortega y Gasset opens
his indictment of the *mass man;* his is not the criticism
of the antidemocrat, but of the believer in the old, liberal, democratic principles of the eighteenth century.
Other social commentators, not antidemocrats either,
bear out some of Ortega y Gasset's contentions. Describing the psychological aspects of *hyperdemocracy,* Erich
Fromm says:

Resembling submissive activity is automaton activity. Here
we do not find dependence on overt authority, but rather on
anonymous authority as it is represented by public opinion, culture patterns, common sense or "science."
. . . A person is not concerned with his life and happiness, but with becoming salable. . . . One has to be in
fashion on the personality market, and in order to be in
fashion one has to know what kind of personality is most in
demand. This knowledge is transmitted in a general way
throughout the whole process of education, from kinder-
garten to college, and implemented by the family. . . . The

meaning which the word *peculiar* has assumed is quite expressive of this attitude. Instead of denoting the greatest achievement of man—that of having developed his individuality—it has become almost synonymous with the word *queer*. The word *equality* has also changed its meaning. The idea that all men are created equal implied that all men have the same fundamental right to be considered as ends in themselves and not as means. Today, equality has become equivalent to interchangeability, and is the very negation of individuality. . . . Equality was conjunctive with difference, but it has become synonymous with "in-difference" and, indeed, indifference is what characterizes modern man's relationship to himself and to others.[3]

Jacques Maritain describes this "indifference" characterizing modern man's relationship to himself and others as that "metallic imperviousness which characterizes so many men and women of our day," and which develops out of "that egotistic and obtrusive self-consciousness which gets rid of shame and anguish only to substitute hardness and insensitiveness."[4] American culture, which prides itself on such catchwords as "individualism," "self-reliance," "independence" has produced its own species of "metallic imperviousness" which indeed, is the very negation of the individualism that is preached. We have been perhaps too eager in recent years to indoctrinate our people with specifically national (and therefore parochial ideals) such as the bastardized Faustian concept of "rugged individualism," so that we have remained unaware of the difference between what Maritain calls *personality* and *individuality*. Personality means "interiority to oneself . . . (which) grows in proportion as the life of reason and freedom dominates over the life of instinct and desire." Individuality "in the strict Aristotelian sense" means *the material ego*, "the displaying of which consists in giving a free hand to the irrational trends of the ego."[5]

> Modern society, in spite of all the emphasis it puts upon happiness, individuality, and self-interest, has taught man to feel that not his happiness (or if we were to use a theological term, his salvation) is the aim of life, but the fulfillment of his duty to work, or his success. Money, prestige, and power have become his incentives and ends. He acts under the illusion that his actions benefit his self-interest, *though he actually serves everything else but the interests of his real self*. Everything is important to him except his life and the art of living. He is for everything except for himself.[6]

It is paradoxical that in a country which puts so much emphasis on liberty and freedom as the keystones of national idealism and national goals, the nonconformist is treated openly with the harshest social brutality. The paradox lies in the fact that this man of "modern society" who has freed his material ego, his individuality, in more ways than ever before, is also more obviously unhappy than ever before. Likewise, the American, the most "socialized," the most overorganized of men, is at one and the same time the loneliest of men. One of the best-known of our popular sociologists, David Riesman, can write a book called *The Lonely Crowd,* the title of which states the essence of the contradiction.

Government and the Average Man

To make a workable definition of democracy, then, we must first get through not only the paradoxes of modern society, but also those many top-of-the-mind generalizations with which most of us, as Americans, have grown up.

For example, ask the proverbial—and yet inevitably elusive—man in the street what he thinks the democratic ideal to be, and he will probably reply, "It's still a free country. Everybody is entitled to his own opinion, and I can say what I please."

Ask him further about the nature of *saying* what he pleases (short of libel, the holding of "communistic" doctrine, or unpopular beliefs) as opposed to *doing* what he pleases, and his answer, if he has one, will be more confusing. It might range anywhere from "I can do what I please as long as I don't hurt anyone," to "What the wife doesn't know and what the boss doesn't know won't hurt them."

If you ask this same common man about his chief aims in life, he might answer in any number of popular aphorisms, including "getting along with people," "being happy" or "finding happiness," "getting ahead in the world," "getting a kick out of life," or "improving myself, improving my mind." That getting ahead in the

vorld may be directly opposed to getting joy from it,
r that improving his mind is possibly antithetical to
ither attaining happiness or getting ahead in the world,
vould not strike the man in the street as particularly
ogent to the discussion. The average American man—
he product of the most extensive mass education ever
een in the world, the product further of the most intense
ystem of mass communication known in the world—
his average man seems to speak wholly in contradic-
ions.

And indeed, this man's life is a series of contradic-
ions; his life as a citizen of a democracy is in itself a
ontradictory process. His first thought on being asked
bout the nature of liberty or of freedom has to do with
he right of free speech: "I can say what I please. It is
till a free country." He can curse the President of the
Jnited States openly; he can curse the Democrats and
Republicans equally, or either one exclusively. How-
ver, he may reach the conclusion that comes to many
"average" men (who, for all their appearance of care-
ul commonness, still hide in some secret corner of the
elf an extreme canniness about the world and its ways,
a sly perverse desire not to believe in all they hear) that
he Republicans and Democrats are really very much
like and that the party out of power constitutes in the
nain—not a deep fundamental opposition, but rather—
a professional rivalry.

To the statement of these contradictions, the average

man most usually replies that "everybody is entitled to
his own opinion." This simple fact has, of course, noth
ing to do with the relative merit of one opinion or an
other—the merit of an opinion formed from knowledge
for example, and of one formed from lack of knowl
edge; the merit of an opinion held after much thought
and experience in contrast to that formed by a man of
no experience and little thought. Nor does the fact that
free speech is law and article of the Constitution of the
United States, bring up in the "average" mind much
reflection on the difference between opinion itself and
the freedom to act upon that opinion—for example, the
"right to revolution." Now the right to act as a private
man "without hurting anyone" is a contradiction of its
own. In the real world it is not possible to act at all with
out in some manner coming into conflict with another
human being or set of human beings: conflict, by its very
nature, implies that somebody is going to get hurt; ac
tion by its very nature, implies conflict.

In actuality, the generalized set of circumstances
lumped too glibly under the term "freedom" has little
to do with the government under which a man lives. If
freedom of choice exists in the world, then it exists as a
reserve in all men, a universal potential. Philosophical-
ly, freedom is the ability of free choice; the freedom to
choose good or evil, or good-and-evil. In the humanistic
terminology of a social critic like Erich Fromm, it is
the choice of fulfilling the creative self, or of alienating

and wronging that self. To John Dewey, freedom is the "creation of the power of self-control"; in Marxist terminology, it is "the recognition of necessity." Jacques Maritain realizes that freedom is the true recognition of personality, of "the interiority to oneself."

> . . . we must never forget that personal freedom itself is at the core of social life, and that a human society is veritably a group of human freedoms which accept obedience and self-sacrifice and a common law for the general welfare. . . . The man and the group are intermingled with each other and they surpass each other in different respects. Man finds himself by subordinating himself to the group, and the group attains its goal only by serving man and by realizing that man has secrets which escape the group and a vocation which is not included in the group.[7]

This secret "which escapes the group" is perhaps the core of the personal capacity for freedom, and since no government can give this secret to man, no government can take it away. Thus, this average man whom we have captured—on any street—is expressing the nature of his paradoxical world when he says that he is "free" because his government grants him freedom. This man is free to get up in the morning by alarm clock, get to work by time clock, take lunch by the restaurant wall clock, and punch out again on the same old time clock. He is free to choose his friends as he pleases; but, as it just happens, his cronies are mostly men of the same general economic and social stamp as himself. He is free to voice any opinion that he likes, but it usually turns out he prefers to voice those feelings which, his "socialized" upbringing has taught him, other men like to hear. He is free to say almost anything he likes about the government—short of wanting to overthrow it—but unless he is active in his local party organization (and a good many average men have neither time nor interest nor energy to be active in this way), the government really does not have much interest in what he, as an individual, says. For that matter, the government is something alien to him; it is too huge to grasp and too complicated to understand. The average man therefore identifies Government with Society; democracy, he firmly believes, is the best of all possible governments (societies) because this is what he has been told. It is also the best because it "gives the common man a chance. Anybody can get ahead in America if they work hard and keep their eye on the ball."

To this "common" man, in actuality, however, the government may resemble the office or the factory in which he works in its hugeness, noncomprehensibility, and complexity and variety of function. The government and the industrial system of which he is a part appear as highly perplexing labyrinths; there are so many byways and so many functionaries for each byway that there seems to be no way possible to pierce to the core of the matter.

This, then, is the nature of the paradox: the American has been told that he is free; he believes that he is free. His success or failure in the world is his "own fault"; his government is "his own" even though he cannot visualize what it is nor how it works. He believes in individualism; on the other hand, he is the sworn enemy of the *different*. (Being different implies, after all, the breakthrough of perversity in oneself, the overt evidence of this perversity in one's life.) This average man must make good at the same time that he cannot be different. He desires education for himself and his children because this means "improving oneself"; on the other hand, he distrusts all intellectuals, that is, all well-educated men, because he suspects them—quite rightly —of tending toward the different, the moody, the strange, the perverse, the critical. He lives in an intricate world dominated by time clocks, stop watches, efficiency checks, the assembly line, and the repeated admonition to keep his eye on some mythical ball—and he calls himself free. He has the greatest industrial plant in the world, so that the world has become for the time being his playground; he is the Poor Little Rich Boy of the whole, wide world. A man was remarking recently that the American in Europe is characterized by his "puppy dog" approach to people. And indeed, the American is warm, friendly, generous—and utterly lonely. As a type, he is "socialized" thoroughly, organized in every imaginable way into every imaginable group—and lonely. His loneliness is that of all oversocialized men; the capacity to participate in many superficial relationships is seldom linked to the ability for making a few deep and truly meaningful contacts with other men.

This is why so many American nonconformists have often run out on America. Anti-intellectualism in this country is almost a profession, and it is to be distinguished from the old and honorable tradition of anti-intellectualism in countries other than America (just as forbidding public or private worship of a given religion is far different from the ancient and honorable tradition of anticlericalism). Whether or not either priests or intellectuals should be elevated to positions of great power in any given society is one question; whether or not they should be allowed to live and breathe freely, is another. The precipitous exit of many an American writer and artist to Europe during the 1920's and 1930's (an exit which continues with renewed force today) is some indication of what these "different" elements seem to be facing in the land of their birth.

In modern American society, the age-old fight of the individual to become fully human (as opposed to the individual who gets ahead or gets along with people) has become more intense than ever. It is more intense, let us say, than in the Athens of Socrates; the institutional matrix of our time is, for one thing, many times more efficient than any city-state system Socrates knew. Modern tyrants have a better chance of absolute power than ever before simply because the weapons and the mass communication facilities at their disposal are so much more extensive than ever before.

As for the United States, not yet threatened by the more obvious forms of tyranny, the devouring quality of the industrial, social, and governmental framework has nevertheless resulted, in many quarters, in a kind of spiritual fascism—what Ortega y Gasset describes as appearing in Europe under direct fascist auspices:

> Under the auspices of Syndicalism and Fascism there appears for the first time in Europe a type of man who does not want to give reasons or to be right, but simply shows himself resolved to impose his opinion. This is the new thing: the right not to be reasonable, the "reason of unreason" . . . that absurd type of human being which I have called "the rebel mass." It is precisely what I mean by having one's soul obliterated, hermetically closed. Here it would be the special case of intellectual hermitism. The individual finds himself already with a stock of ideas. He decides to content himself with them and to consider himself intellectually complete. As he feels the lack of nothing outside himself, he settles down definitely amid his mental furniture. Such is the mechanism of self-obliteration. . . . Once for all, he accepts the stock of commonplaces, prejudices, fag-ends of ideas or simply empty words which chance has piled up within his mind, and with a boldness only explicable by his ingenuousness, is prepared to impose them everywhere.[8]

Individualism, Real or Imagined

At this point it is legitimate to ask, "Why this strange contradiction between the expressed national idea of individualism and freedom, and the reality of the matter? Has the American always been this way?"

First of all, our national history is unique. There have been mass migrations before in the history of man, or deportations by force, but these migrations and deportations have been forgotten. They have been forgotten because they have left few talebearers. People wandering from one part of Europe to another after the fall of the Roman Empire (as after any great break-up of an old order) usually melted into new segments, new formations; and their origins were forever left behind. Likewise, mass deportations of whole populations from one area to another erased—in most cases, within one generation—all ties with the old language and the old culture. One of the rare exceptions to this rule is Judaism, which has been kept both religiously and culturally alive throughout generations of dispersal of individual Jews. But the Jews constitute an historical freak.

In so far as the memory of their mass migration has survived, the Americans, too, are historically odd. The American ideals of freedom and of individualism which seemed so strangely vestigial in 1955, were frontier ideals. The men who settled that frontier have long since taken on the sweetness and sentimentality which the passage of time and idealization tend to give. But these people in actuality were rebels, outcasts, lawbreakers (or at least law resenters), claustrophobes in search of elbowroom and an escape from Other Men altogether—difficult, seamy, moody, and often inarticulate men. They were, in the best tradition of twentieth century existentialism, *alienated* men; or they were, in the best traditions of piracy, freebooters and entrepreneurs.

The frontier, by its very nature, was antithetical to all class distinctions. It was the reality of the frontier which gave support to the social ideal that all men should have *equality of opportunity*. The other ideal which differentiates the American democratic concept of government from other kinds is a much older one: the *equality of all men before law*. No medieval society could have originated the idea of social equality because the medieval world rested on the concept of each man in his place, and a place for each man; in addition, the medieval structure was based on serf labor. Though the idea of equality before law is—in both the real and the proverbial senses—as old as the Greeks, the idea of equality of opportunity could never have been originated in Athens because the society in which Socrates preached and Plato taught was based on slave labor. The French, in their famous revolution, anticipated but could not implement the idea of freedom of social mobility. The short-lived desire for liberty, equality, and fraternity culminated in the Napoleonic Wars and a resurrection of the old class society.

The Americans had one advantage over the French, and that advantage was the frontier. On any frontier, the classless society is almost a reality, because the family name, the prestige, the fame, even the money which a man leaves behind him is not so important as the ability to survive which he brings with him. The frontier—the exact experience of the frontier and the rumbles of legend it still leaves in American life—is one reason for the paradoxical nature of American idealism, and the "lonely crowd" aspect of American life.

Oliver Twist Versus Huckleberry Finn

W. H. Auden compares the English with the American concept of what society should be by examining two famous small-boy heroes from either culture, Oliver Twist and Huckleberry Finn:

> When we close *Oliver Twist*, we know that all the friends he has made during his adventures will remain his friends for life, but when we finish *Huckleberry Finn* we feel that even Jim, with whom he has enjoyed a friendship more intense than any of Oliver's, is going to be left behind the moment they get back to Missouri. The conclusions of the two novels draw a sharp contrast between the English and the American daydream:
>
> "Mr. Brownlow went on from day to day, filling the mind of his adopted child with stores of knowledge, and becoming attached to him more and more, as his nature developed itself, and showed the thriving seeds of all he wished to become."
>
> [versus]
>
> "I reckon I got to light out for the Territory ahead of the rest, because Aunt Sally she's going to adopt me and sivilize me, and I can't stand it. I been there before."[9]

What Oliver Twist has been looking for all his life—a nice home, a father, stability, the chance to become a respectable citizen—is precisely what Huckleberry Finn does not want (and indeed what the Wandering American never, in his heart of hearts, seems to want either). Oliver Twist lives with a set of rules which fix Right and Duty as inevitable and unchanging verities. But

> . . . nothing in Huck's past experience can tell him what he should do, and he cannot draw from his choice any general conclusions as to how he or others ought to behave in further situations: *morally he must always be an amateur.* Whatever Clemens' views on slavery may have been, from Mark Twain one can only draw two conclusions: either a relativist one, that every form of society, slave-owning or free or blood-feuding, is a way of life which is agreeable to its members and which, therefore, an outsider has no right to judge; or an anarchist one, that all public social values are false and useless to the individual in discovering what is true, *which he can only discover by himself.* . . . All human affections, it seems to say, are the creatures of some occasion and perish with it; the strongest tie in time becomes a burden; *love and freedom are incompatible.*[10]

Huckleberry Finn, then, is the original spirit of the frontier; he lives without tradition; he lives by the maxim "Live and let live; if I let them alone they should let me alone to find my way." Society as such may be more often wrong than right, as it is wrong in making the Negro, Jim, a slave, and as it is wrong in attempting to hunt Jim down when he escapes from slavery. But so-

ciety does not know what it does; it is blind; it simply
exists; and in existing and being blind it is neither moral
nor immoral. Only the individual can make moral
choices. Society may be respectable like Aunt Sally, or
oppressive like the slave owners, or cruel and wrong-
headed like the blood-feuding clans, but it is almost
never to be considered as a standard to which the just
can repair. Rather, society is a powerful and impassive
force; when an individual like Huck Finn wants hon-
estly to search for his soul, he must get away from society; he must circumvent it, outwit, outrun it, or come
to terms with it in temporary fashion. In defending the
Negro slave, Jim, Huck comes into conflict with all of
Southern society, and his awareness of this fact makes
him wary of all respectable people.

> The best of Mark Twain's fiction is, historically, the first
> mature realization in our literature of a conflict between the
> assumptions of democracy and the limitations of democracy.
> Between the ideal of freedom and the nature of man.
>
> The damned human race is displayed with derision and
> abhorrence, yet this is on the ground that it has *fallen short
> of its own decencies* . . . it is the essence of what Mark
> Twain had to say that the hero is a Negro slave. It is also a
> vindication not only of freedom, but of loyalty and decency,
> kindness and courage; and it is the essence of Mark Twain
> that this vindication is made by means of a boy who is a
> spokesman of the folk mind and whom experience has taught
> wariness and skepticism. Like all great novels *Huckleberry
> Finn* moves on many levels of significance, but it describes a

flight and a struggle for freedom, and the question it turns on is a moral question.[11]

Huckleberry Finn, too, is a pragmatist in the American way; he is a moral amateur because all his actions are based upon the exigencies of the moment, and not upon a philosophy of conduct. He must cut through the barriers of his own wariness and those other barriers erected by society in order to follow the way of the heart, and to become a friend of Jim, the slave. Like Huck, the American as a national type is more willing to trust his emotions than any reasoned interpretation of conduct. The profound anti-intellectualism that cuts through the American grain is not simply a result of what Ortega y Gasset calls *hyperdemocracy;* it is based upon the assumption that the heart will always be at war with reason; it is the idea that the judgments of reasoned men are hard, cold things. "Experience is the best teacher," says the man-in-the-street, meaning that pragmatism is the best philosophy and that theoretical knowledge should be viewed with suspicion. This is one of the reasons that so many Americans appear to Europeans to be impulsive, generous, and not overly thoughtful. In older cultures kindness is looked upon as a minor virtue; in America it is a major one. The European has lived in a tradition which formalizes the varied springs of men's hostilities; he is more aware of the ironic fact that kindness, too, may result in evil. All traditionalists know that this pragmatic heart in which the American puts so much trust, can also run amuck. In one of his novels, Graham Greene has a whiskey priest say to the saintly anticlerical who is going to kill him:

> Oh, well, perhaps when you're my age you'll come to know the heart's an untrustworthy beast. The mind is too, but it doesn't talk about love. Love. And a girl puts her head under the water or the child's strangled, and the heart all the time says love, love.[12]

Man alone and apart from all society, all tradition, is a recurrent theme in American literature. Again and again in Ernest Hemingway's novels the heroes are men divorced, alienated, or outcast from society; the dark novels of Melville are concerned with men who are outcasts, renegades, or who, like Pierre, a typical Melvillian hero, are intent on a search for truth which ends in madness. William Faulkner, one of the few contemporary American writers who has a concept of men and women acting within a framework of cultural tradition, presents that tradition as decadent and invalid. C. Hartley Grattan, commenting on James Farrell, says:

> Farrell believes that man is the victim of the institutional arrangements of society because "the powers of the individual will are weaker than the forces of social circumstance. . . . " If man can change the institutional complex in which he is entangled, then he will achieve freedom, emerge from the Kingdom of Necessity into the Kingdom of Freedom. . . . Social institutions make a man, at bottom admirable, into a depressing slob. . . . That man can accomplish his own rescue is axiomatic in Farrell's thinking. . . . [13]

It is possible that the heavy emphasis in radio, films, and TV on the gangster and the gangster's affairs is not without cause. On one hand the gangster represents a kind of degraded Huckleberry Finn tradition; he is the man daringly, boldly, openly at odds with society. He is the freebooter, the robber baron, as much as Jay Gatsby, the romantic bootlegger in F. Scott Fitzgerald's novel, *The Great Gatsby*.

> The last two pages of the book make overt Gatsby's embodiment of the American dream as a whole by identifying his attitude with the awe of the Dutch sailors when, "for a transitory enchanted moment," they found "something commensurate to (their) capacity for wonder" in the "fresh, green breast of the new world." Though this commitment to the wonder and enchantment of a dream is qualified by the dream's unreality, by its "year by year receding before us," the dream is still the book's only positive good. . . . [14]

There were people—and respectable people—who dipped handkerchiefs in the blood of John Dillinger when that famous gangster was shot down by police following a long and startling career. Could it be that John Dillinger was on the nether or illegal side of a tradition exemplified by such old-time respectable freebooters as John Jacob Astor and Jay Gould.

Tradition in the American Way

Whereas in other countries tradition is a warm, human thing, a motherly receptacle of most virtues and many

vices, in America tradition is something traditionally to
be avoided. The business of tradition has always been
to present to men a philosophic structure which recreates
the things that *are* in a satisfying, livable pattern, and
which outlines the things that *should be*. The American,
however, identifies tradition with the institutional matrix
which is inclined, in Farrell's terminology, to make him
into a "depressing slob." The time-clock heart which
keeps his great industrial system alive is indeed a depressing fact. On this issue, the European criticism of
America is too well known to be anything but trite. The
American, says the European, is so obsessed with time,
with rushing from place to place in an endless circle of
quite often meaningless events, that he cannot keep
heart's time; he does not dare to look at the world around
him and receive gratification from observance and speculation.

It is perhaps in this truism, however, that the heart
of the paradox lies. The seventeenth, eighteenth, and
early nineteenth century American was not devoid of
tradition; the ideas of government and of liberty under
law which the early settlers brought with them were
wholly European and derivative. And yet the westward
movement across the continent was carried on by people
who, for the most part, feared involvement in the cum-
bersome, comfortable, and often stultifying weight of
any institutional framework. These were the people who,
in frontier terminology, prided themselves on being "in-

dependent as a hog on ice"; they feared and avoided the influence of Other People; freedom to them was a geographical thing, a physical thing, a thing of space and virgin land. Freedom was loneliness and equality of opportunity.

In contrast, the American of the present day is indeed the most "socialized," overorganized individual on earth. But even though this is true, the ghosts of those frontier boastings and of the Gatsbian freebooter's dream hang over us in the ideological air. The American imagination is a divided thing, torn between a past which, within the span of two generations, has already receded into the golden haze of myth, and the intensely institutional framework of the mass society of the present.

Three major factors have combined to bring about the complex institutional framework in which we presently live: mass technology, mass education, and the closing of the frontier. There were, in one sense, two frontiers. One of them was closed in the 1870's, when it became apparent that there was little free land left in the West. The second closed during the 1920's, with the enactment of restrictive legislation against immigration. When Woodrow Wilson vetoed the literacy test for immigrants, he was one of the last of the American statesmen to stand against immigration quotas. His veto was given on the grounds that the American people were, by and large, silent on the issue, and that the "right of political asylum has brought to this country many a man of noble character and elevated purpose who was marked as an outlaw in his own less fortunate land."[15]

In this way the great and generous boast of America, the famous boast engraved on the Statue of Liberty, "Give me your toiling masses, your poor . . . " was forever finished, become economically unfeasible, socially impossible, geographically at an end. Whereas the earlier settlers were lured to the West by the promise of the possibility of free land and personal anarchism, the later pioneers—Poles, Italians, Lithuanians, Russians, Armenians, Jews—came to a country where the virgin forests had been replaced by an asphalt jungle. Torn from their language and culture by the promise of political freedom or equal opportunity, the later pioneers faced a terrifying wilderness of city streets, slums, sweatshops, all the crudities attendant upon the growing pains of an industrial civilization. If it had taken courage for frontiersmen to face the forests and the Indians, it took an even more intense kind of bravery for the later immigrants to plunge headlong into a jungle of cheerless coal towns, industrial wastes, and a struggle for existence dominated by sheer cash values.

These latter-day immigrants were needed—not to settle the land—but to mine the coal, build the factories, work the machine treadles, provide cheap labor on the railroads. And each wave of migration was faced with ostracism of one sort or another. In the 1840's and '50's in the Midwest there were advertisements for jobs which read "Irishmen and dogs need not apply." Jacob A. Riis says in his book, *How the Other Half Lives* (1890):

> The German ragpicker of thirty years ago, quite as low in the scale as his Italian successor, is the thrifty tradesman or prosperous farmer today. . . . As emigration from east to west follows the latitude, so does the foreign influx in New York distribute itself along certain well-defined lines that waver and break only under the strongest pressure of a more gregarious race or the encroachments of inexorable business.[16]

The Irish were successors to the Germans as "low men" on the social totem pole; Southern Europeans and Slavs succeeded the Irish. Meanwhile, on the West Coast, the Chinese, the Japanese, and in the end, the Okies, were all lured to the harvest fields only to be left in penury when the harvests or the railroad building were done with.[17] The most recent examples of "lower men" replacing the old "low men" on the totem pole are two groups: the Mexican wetbacks, who swim across the Rio Grande on the hunt for jobs in the United States, and who are sent packing back across the border as illegal entrants when they are no longer needed as the cheapest of labor; and the Puerto Ricans, who, as citizens of the United States, cannot be sent packing. The Puerto Ricans in New York took the place hitherto held by Negroes on the economic and social scale, and became part of a

spreading slum pattern, "Spanish Harlem." Still other
Puerto Ricans came to Chicago, where language barriers and social ostracism again set them apart.

These two frontiers, then—the geographical and later
the technological one—had the effect of attracting and
partially absorbing a mass of differing population
groups. The American bloodstream only partially ab-
sorbed and never digested its many component parts because "the great melting pot" has never really done
what it was advertised to do—it has not melted. In any
large city in the United States can be found pockets of
resistance to assimilation—the Chinatowns, the Jewish
and Negro ghettoes, the Polish, Irish, Italian neighborhoods. Some of these groups actively resist being melted
in order to keep strong ethnic and cultural ties; some,
most notably Negroes, are inevitably forced by prejudice and the barriers of caste, into segregation. Those
groups who desire to keep their own cultural base have
good reason to do so. In America there is no primary
pattern into which any minority can melt (presuppos-
ing that they are allowed to melt at all) without losing
something in favor of something considerably less. What
any minority man who succeeds in melting seems to lose
is a kind of uniqueness, a color all his own. What he
gains is most usually the attribute of colorlessness, a
membership in the local Rotarian club, and a voice
speaking the same patriotic or businesslike phrases as
those of a thousand other voices around him.

The Democratic Hero—Have We One?

The only factor which ties all Americans together is not a cultural but an ideological one, nationalism—nationalism, and a word which has come to be used interchangeably in America with patriotism (and which has come, in addition, to mean all things to all men): democracy. Now democracy, of all the political systems as yet in use, is the most subtle and the most complicated. It demands the ability to compromise and the ability to see many issues at once. Understood correctly, it means a system of diffused power spread in interrelated fashion over a jigsaw of pressure groups.

Thus the ideal democratic hero is a man much more cautious than Beowulf about drawing his sword against dragons, for the dragon may have some good in him after all (and further, the dragon might represent a significant pressure group). On the other hand, the ideal democratic hero must have a face of conviction, a principle in mind (for otherwise he would be no hero at all, but an opportunist). The ideal democratic hero must, as F. Scott Fitzgerald succinctly phrased it, "hold two opposed ideas in his mind at once." The ideal democratic hero might very well be a combination of Huckleberry Finn (that precise blend of suspicion of humanity and love of humanity), Will Rogers (who used the mother-wit of his suspicion to create the folk-wit of love), Franklin Delano Roosevelt (who betrayed his patrician an-

cestry by becoming a politician), and Henry Adams
(who bemoaned the fact that all his life his patrician upbringing gave him too much mother-wit to be useful in
politics).

No such hero, of course, has appeared upon the
scene. The actual and official hero is a man with a Rotarian heart and the face of George Washington. Of
this hero it is demanded that he absorb all colors and all
cultures, so that in the end he has no color and no culture at all. His emotional tone is perhaps dominantly
middle class (because it is to a large extent the middle
class in this country which, though not necessarily wanting to *include* all races, religions, and cultures, nevertheless wistfully desires to *make over* all races, religions,
and cultures into its own image).

Class in the Classless Society

In our country, where a great many people want to be
"just like everybody else," the wish cannot be father to
the act because there is no truly representative standard
to which the just can repair. The attempt to create such
a standard has been made largely through a free mass
education. And it becomes more and more true that the
attempt to give everyone in our society a minimum
amount of education, has been carried through by the
middle class, through the middle class, and finally, for
the middle class. One of the basic reasons for this fact
is that for more than a century Americans have viewed

education—not as an end in itself but—as a means by which their children might compete for the social and financial rewards at the end of the rainbow.

> For more than a hundred years the American people have had an abiding faith in education as a means of promoting social mobility, of maintaining a society essentially free from class and caste. . . . Jefferson gave concrete expression to it in his plan for education in Virginia and it was fostered by the social ideals of the more or less classless society of each succeeding West. . . . In time, social mobility came to be the essence of American democracy; the way to place, power, and social esteem, so it was felt, should be open to youth of ability and energy regardless of inheritance. Indeed, place and power should, in great degree, be redistributed at the end of each generation.[18]

The frontier and the idea of the *melting pot* where all men might find equal opportunity were one and the same thing; a little later the idea of an impartial and free educational system became a kind of substitute for the frontier and the melting pot. Even before 1920, when immigration became a matter of quotas, observers of the American scene saw the handwriting on the wall: the increasing concentration of wealth in the hands of a few; the political and commercial expansion of the United States into foreign areas overseas; the increase of industrial strife and ethnic tensions. As the handwriting on the wall became more obvious to most thoughtful Americans, many true believers in the American dream gave way to panic or despair. Americans who had pro-

claimed too glibly (and dreamed too wistfully) of the
"classless society" realized, by the early 1920's, that
the United States was not this in fact. The ghost of this
generous American dream expired in its first phase with
the exhaustion of free land in the West; the second
phase was shaken, perhaps to death, by the Depression
of the 1930's and the dawning realization that the Great
Experiment in mass education might not be able to provide equal opportunity either. By the 1940's American
educators could publicly announce the aims of the present American educational system to be the function of a
class society:

> First, the school system serves the children of different classes
> in different ways; and second, the school system selects a
> minority and trains them for social mobility. The one as-
> pect of selectivity operates to preserve the status system, and
> the other aspect operates to help children secure the re-
> wards for climbing within the status system.[19]

Now such aims—the security of a status system—remain
impossible for many Americans either to like or to ap-
prove of. The theory, for those Americans brought up on
the ideal of Abraham Lincoln studying by candlelight in
a log cabin, may be difficult to accept; the reality of the
matter is difficult for realistic men *not* to accept. The
reality means that the avowed aim of much of American
education is to provide opportunity for the *select few* to
"secure the rewards of climbing within the status system." And since the Great Depression, some educational

commentators have begun to ask the question which is
so horrifying to True Believers in the classless promise
of the New World: perhaps we are selecting *too many*;
now when too many people in a society are led to expect
too much and they subsequently don't get it, doesn't
something ominous follow?

> If too many people are led to expect to rise in the world,
> they become a threat to social cohesion. . . . I believe we
> must seriously inquire whether we are not encouraging
> many more boys and girls to hope for social mobility through
> high school and college attendance than can conceivably find
> professional and managerial positions in the social struc-
> ture. . . . I believe that our society would be in a healthier
> condition if the number of boys and girls who hope to rise
> in the world through high school were reduced. Please no-
> tice that I have not said that we should reduce the number
> of boys and girls attending high school and college. We are
> not producing too many college graduates for the positions
> acceptable to them. . . . We do not in this country have the
> serious problem of the unemployed scholar that plagued
> half the continents of Europe during the late 1920's and
> 1930's. In European countries, with a social structure more
> mature and more rigid than ours, the secondary school and
> the university were practically the only avenues of social
> mobility.[20]

There is no more room at the top! This fear of vanish-
ing *Lebensraum* is especially terrifying because it is
new to Americans, and because it has been for so long
a culturally inadmissible idea. The rigidity which Hav-

ighurst suggests as an educational way out of this inadmissible idea sounds like the cry of a man in terror; because Havighurst can only suggest that the first and last aim of American education should be the classification of people into more usable social categories: fewer people in the "higher" managerial positions; more people content with being garage mechanics and high school graduates.

> The high school program would be designed to make the great majority of students satisfied with their present status in the social structure. . . . It is important to recognize that when I speak of satisfaction with present status in the social structure I do not mean satisfaction with present economic standards of living, for I believe it is desirable to raise the general economic standard of the lower-status groups. The standard of living may be raised for an entire group without the individual members of the group rising in social status. Where I speak of satisfaction with present status, I mean status with respect to one's neighbors and fellow-citizens. I would make an exception of the people in the lowest socio-economic level. Their children should not be educated to be satisfied with their present individual positions. But their children seldom get to high school.[21]

Havighurst seems to view with equanimity the prospect of relegating "their" children who "seldom get to high school" to the ranks of the permanently uneducated. And in essence his diagnosis of the "way out" means consigning a "great majority of students" to a strictly class education, that is, an inferior or indifferent education. Out of that "more mature and more rigid" European social structure of which Havighurst speaks, there comes far more awareness of what indoctrination in *class* values can lead to and, quite often, a more realistic idea of how to deal with it. As an Englishman speaking to other Englishmen, Alfred North Whitehead says:

> You may perhaps, by some great reform, obviate the worst kind of sweated labor and the insecurity of employment. But you can never greatly increase average incomes. On that side all hope of Utopia is closed to you. It would, however, require no very great effort to use your schools to produce a population with some love of music, some enjoyment of drama, and some joy in beauty of form and color. We could also provide means for the satisfaction of these emotions in the general life of the population. . . . Today we deal with herded town populations, reared in a scientific age. I have no doubt that unless we can meet the new age with new methods, to sustain for our populations the life of the spirit, sooner or later, amid some savage outbreak of defeated longings, the fate of Russia will be the fate of England.[22]

Now here Whitehead speaks directly—even brutally —to the real problem of mass education, that is, to the existence of *herded town populations.* He understands that what defeats men is not their failure to rise within or through or around any given set of "class" lines, but rather, the continued sense of failure as human beings. This kind of failure in becoming human, becoming a man, is the only real kind of failure there is. And this failure of the self in fulfilling *interiority to itself* (the kind of failure which Fromm and Maritain have described), multiplied a hundred thousand times, is the real threat to social cohesion.

Socialization, a Term for Conformity

At its very worst, American education has become that process of socialization by which the perverse in all men could be filed down to the accepting and acceptable. In the terminology of many educators this became nothing less than education for mediocrity and conformity.

> The socialized person must embrace the value system of his group, but this does not mean that he can never challenge the beliefs of others. *Reform does not require rebellion.* The successful reformer is ordinarily one who shares most of the values of the people of his time. . . . Our group accepts the social theory that it is unhealthy to require everyone to think alike, though we too sometimes make life uncomfortable for nonconformers.[23]

Apart from the fact that reform has always, in actuality, required a great deal of will stemming from rebellion in its purest forms, this socialization educator's feeling that "we too sometimes make life uncomfortable for nonconformers" is one of the most interesting of understatements. The understatement illustrates one of the first fears from which all socialization educators begin: the fear of a heterogeneous population group. A homogeneous society, such as that of the English, would seem

to have the advantage of tolerating—or even of wel-
coming—the eccentric. Since everyone starts from a
common value system, great deviations c_n be allowed
for; the cultural base remains wide enough to create the
necessary climate of acceptance.

In contrast, the horror of race rioting is never very
far from the consciousness of the man who undertakes
mass education in the United States; he attempts to do
what he can about it with his little packet of Core Values,
among which can always be counted the value and duty
of Brotherhood. Now the emphasis on Brotherhood in
our public schools is usually a soapy and ineffective
affair; it is so because it has been generally innocuous.
Since racial equality is a touchy subject in schools both
North and South, the general tendency has been avoidance of the real issues in favor of the hygienic idea of
"co-operation" and "toleration," an abstract ideal which
usually boils down to a kind of uneasy co-existence with
people of different ethnic and religious origins.

An exhaustive study of seven major school systems by Bra-
meld revealed that administrative policies in American school
systems range from a "direct, forthright attack upon minority problems, through a twilight zone of uncertainty, to an
opposite policy almost completely opposed to direct attack
of any kind. . . . In one of our largest manufacturing cities
with a population of more than one million inhabitants,
which possessed a good philosophy of intergroup education
on the top administrative level, about one-half of all school

principals believed that the best answer to the question of how to deal with the interracial issue is "Don't bring it out."[24]

Teachers who should by rights have been "leaders rather than followers" could not accomplish much "against the opposition of the community on which [they were] financially and politically dependent"; prejudiced parents were "in an excellent position to nullify gains made in schools"; and in general, "the average teacher shares the traditional prejudice of his community," and even though he is "often especially indoctrinated to suppress his own prejudiced attitudes in the classroom," such suppressed attitudes will out.[25]

One of the greatest problems of a democratic society is to teach its children the recognition of freedom. And among other things, the recognition of freedom means the recognition of difference: the right of One's interior personality to develop apart from the Others'; the right of the Others' to develop apart from One. This recognition has not been taught; indeed, most educational theory in America today operates under the illusion that students must be adjusted to some mythical norm. Even on the simplest levels of the recognition and acceptance of differences—that is, in the area of our ethnic and racial problems—our education has for the most part not been a success.

However, the fear of decreasing social cohesion which motivates our educators is very real; that they have not been able to deal with it in a virile and direct manner is

needs of a good number of its citizens—has no real need to list Core Values at all. The English public school, whatever its manifest faults, at least produced a good number of citizens whose values were so well internalized that nobody needed to mention the obvious. It is still true that no traditionalized Englishman mentions his philosophy of life—at least not in public, and never without blushing. We may visualize the American public school adolescent, on the other hand, as a properly socialized product, rattling off his Core Values like a regular turbine whenever asked: "I believe in the dignity of man, the principle that all men are created equal," and so on.

By tradition the American has been a nonideological animal, a political innocent. His cynicism about politics is proverbial. His cynicism and naïveté are two sides of the same coin: he is wary of being taken in at the same time that he dismisses those who might take him in as "politicians" and bombasts. It was not wise to have expected of the American soldier—easygoing, wisecracking, cynical, politically unsophisticated, mechanically proficient, and practical—that, come the Second World War, he should suddenly become a fanatic in defense of a religious cause. It is precisely one of the great advantages—and disadvantages—of the democratic mind that, whether well- or ill-trained, it does not easily become fanatic. Until recently there existed a democratic tradition of antimilitarism. The famed and recalcitrant iso-

lationism of the American Midwest was partly based on
this antimilitaristic tradition, and partly on more can-
tankerous ideas: fear of the outsider (represented by
other nations of the world), and a mixture of cynicism,
political ignorance, and a desire not to "nose around in
other people's business." Today, the Midwest accepts the
military regularity of life—that is, the inevitability of
their sons going to the army for the prescribed two years
—but the acceptance is without zeal. Fanaticism is *not*
either the virtue or the vice of the democratic temperament, but apathy sometimes is.

It may be the very vague and yet exclusive neutrality
of this emotional tone which accounts in large part for
the distinct change in the traditional attitude of the present older generation in regard to the present younger
generation. It has been noted before that there is much
less thunder about "what the younger generation is coming to" and much more wonder about what it is not coming to. It is middle-aged men and women who call the
younger group "The Silent Generation." And even with
the various purges of educators, college professors still
note with some surprise that they are more radical, more
ready to take a chance, more ready to explore possibilities, than the great majority of their students.

It is not "softness" which causes this new generation
to desire security above all other ends in life; rather, it
is the fear of the unknown—fear of the ups and downs of
an unpredictable economic system, fear of wars the de-

claring and brewing of which seem more and more to be out of any man's control. The American of the so-called Silent Generation has perhaps taken his socialization lessons to heart; whereas all cultures make some effort to "socialize" their youth in those paths which are most useful, or at least most traditional, the Silent Generation has been brought up in the kind of environment in which *socialization has become an end in itself.* We can understand how the twin and paradoxical goals of individualism and "getting along with people" came to exist side by side only when we realize that a large section of the American public once read Dale Carnegie with deep earnestness. And yet, actually, at one time Carnegie lifted those machinations which Machiavelli once labeled scientifically and by their right names to the status of a mass substitute for religion. Thus co-operation with other men became synonymous with hidden aggression against them; wholesomeness became another word for innocuousness; and democracy itself another word for mediocrity.

The basic theme of the usual program of education is motivation toward success. . . . Such motivation is intrinsically unsound in its palpable impossibility of attainment. . . . Most people do not know how to fail—that is, they do not know how to meet failure without recourse to a variety of abnormal reactions, such as escapes, evasions, rationalizations, or unusual compensations. . . . If our educational system could inculcate the attitude that certain types of failure are inevitable and that the purpose of failure may, perhaps, be to learn and to stimulate activity, it is quite possible that the number of neurotic and hostile persons would be reduced.[26]

The Everyman of American society is Willie Loman, hero of "The Death of a Salesman," whose tragedy consisted in the fact that he could not, until he was too old and it was too late, even recognize the existence of tragedy. Willie Loman finally broke his heart on the fact that not every man in America could "make" the top. Other societies treated this fact as a matter of course, but all the great socializing agencies of Willie Loman's life had taught him that *it was his own fault* if he didn't "make the grade."

Man—Mortal and Human

Thus, the one thing which a great deal of American life and a good deal of American education—both formal and informal—has failed to do, is to educate for tragedy —the ultimate tragedy of man. Tragedy to Willie Loman meant the failure of his individual ambitions; it was a shameful rather than an inevitable or a sublime thing. This is why so many popular books in America—many of which pretend to be religious—play upon the one idea, Everyone Can Have Happiness, Everyone Can Have Success, Everyone Can Be Loved. It is because of such books and of the almost ridiculously false optimism of the climate behind them, that American soldiers might very well be forced to take refuge in cynicism against the insistent declaration of the Core Values to which they were supposed to give verbal belief. It is because of this climate that Willie Loman never really comes to realize his great mistake to have been not the failure to *make the grade*, but the failure to understand that living the good life is always and everywhere more important than making any grade imposed by any temporal set of institutions or societies. In the words of Robert Redfield:

> . . . the end of man's existence is not co-operation. It is not even safety. It is to live up to the fullest possibilities of humanity. And man is human only as long as he knows the good and shares that knowing with those to whom he is, in humanity, bound. . . . The question, "Can we all, on this earth, get along together?" is, of course, an immensely important question because it has to be answered successfully if we are to ask any other. But even more important is the question, "Why should we try to do so? What should we work for, live for? What is the good life?"[27]

The American temper has always been pragmatic, practical, optimistic, and, in the lingo of the salesman, "forward-looking." But behind the pressing cultural need of Americans to look always on the "bright side of things" is the lonely, the peculiar melancholy of Huckleberry Finn, of Melville's *Confidence Man*. It appears difficult for the American in his art or his literature to transmute that melancholia akin to madness into the catharsis of high tragedy. In a sense, the very virtues in-

herent in his pragmatism force him into an avoidance of
the bigger question: "What is the good life?" Americans
have answered too glibly and in immediate terms: "The
good life means providing the most goods for the most
people, and distributing those goods in the most efficient
way possible."

The present-day American and the present-day Russian alike seem to share this belief in the unending progress of man toward some ultimate goal. In whatever ways
communism and democracy differ, it would seem that
the ways of life of the two peoples focus more on the
question of "How is it done?" rather than "Why should
it be done and to what end?"

On this score both the American and the Russian appear to be avoiding the tragedy of man—the fact that all
men must die; the fact that all men, while living, must
attempt to some extent the impossible, and in attempting
the impossible are doomed, of course, to failure. Both
the revolutionary Communist and the American go-
getter seem to want to avoid the true condition of man—
not because of materialism, the sin with which they most
often charge each other—but rather, because of an excess
of idealism. *Life can become so good,* runs their premise,
that we shall no longer have to recognize tragedy as the
basis of man's life.

The ironic paradox here lies in the fact that these victims of dynamic idealism, these priests of infinite progress, have created in our time a monster to outdo all

monsters, a tragedy to end all tragedies: the atom bomb, and the possibility of generic death.

In this setting, the bewilderment of the American of our generation can be more easily understood. His bewilderment parallels that of the early revolutionary Bolshevik who, in wanting to destroy the old evil icons, awakens one day to the installation of new and more terrible forms of enslavement. The American idealist, likewise, had wanted only good; he had declared that the end result of the greatest industrial production plant of the modern world would be the elimination of starvation all over the world.

It might be well, therefore, that we re-examine the democratic ideal and the democratic practice in the light of the mushroom cloud over Hiroshima; for the end result of pragmatism at Hiroshima was that America, indeed, did not know what it had done.

Chapter 2

I hope that we shall . . . crush in its birth the aristocracy of our monied corporations which dare already to challenge our government to a trial of strength and bid defiance to the laws of the country.
—THOMAS JEFFERSON

The Time-Clock Heart

MONOPOLY or centralization of economic power seems to be the order of the day in business and industry, in spite of the fact that democracy in practical operation should spread power over as wide an area of society as possible. Automation, the operation of factories and businesses by electronic power, brings into today's picture the Second Industrial Revolution. What is the American answer to the moral dilemma which faces both capitalist and workingman, torn between the downswing of a peacetime economy and the upswing of a wartime economy? Automation itself is a paradox which offers the choice of a heaven or a hell on earth. Man, technically free to explore the universe, is smothered by the impersonality of the very institutions he has been able to create through technology. How shall he find moral ballast? Have both management and labor overlooked the fact that the fundamental cause of unrest is the desire of individual workers to be treated as human beings, not as commodities on the market?

The Trend Toward Monopoly

The manager of the Ford foundry in Cleveland gives us, in the 1950's, the Shape of Things to Come: "Ours is the only foundry in the world where the molding sand used to make castings is never touched by human hands except maybe out of curiosity."[1] Frederick Jackson Turner noted the shape of this same future, which is even now receding into our past:

> The iron, the coal, and the cattle of the country have all fallen under the domination of a few great corporations with allied interests, and by the rapid combination of the important railroad systems and steamship lines, in concert with these same forces, even the breadstuffs and the manufactures of the nation are to some degree controlled in the same way.[2]

In 1935 thirty corporations had assets of a billion dollars or more; two of these corporations had assets greater than the assessed valuation of all the property in each of thirty-eight states. That is, only ten states had "in their respective larders property valued at more than the assets of each of these two corporations."[3]

In 1947, according to the Federal Trade Commission, 46 per cent of all the manufacturing property, plant, and equipment used in the United States was owned by the 113 largest corporations in the country. One hundred corporations received two-thirds of the dollar volume of war contracts during the Second World War; in the

Korean war, *fifty* corporations got two-thirds of the dollar volume. According to the Statistical Abstracts of 1952, there were 2,462 mergers in mining and manufacturing from 1940 to 1947, precisely double the mergers which occurred between 1920 and 1928.

But this centralization of economic power among the largest corporate interests has not changed the distribution of income in the United States, a distribution which is essentially the same today as it was in 1910, when the upper fifth of income units received 46.2 per cent of money income, and the lowest fifth 8.3 per cent. In the 1950 census, it came out that the highest fifth of income families and unrelated individuals received 47 per cent of the total income, as contrasted to the 3 per cent received by the lowest fifth. Taxes, often suggested as a cure for the fact that the poor seem to be getting poorer all the time, don't seem to have much effect; in 1950 the highest tenth of the income units received 29 per cent of all money income before taxes; after taxes they got 27 per cent. Meanwhile, the second highest tenth received 15 per cent before taxes—and 15 per cent after. The top-heaviness of this ratio is further increased by the fact that 6/10 of 1 per cent of all American families own 80 per cent of all publicly held corporation stock.

No American who thinks at all about the changing face of democracy in his country can neglect to consider these statistics. As we have said, a pragmatic definition of democracy means the diffusion of power over as wide an area in society as possible. Rather than diffusion, these figures point to an intense centralization of economic power in our society. It is quite implausible for Soviet apologists to protest that the people of the Soviet Union can have "economic democracy" at the cost of "political democracy." It is equally implausible to suggest that Americans can have political democracy without some form of economic decentralization of power, because in no period of human history has it ever been possible to separate political from economic power.

Automation and the American Economy

Economic centralization becomes even more apparent in our country as we enter the Second Industrial Revolution. The First Industrial Revolution replaced animal and human muscle power with steam- and electric-powered machines; automation uses electronic devices to replace human regulation and control of machines. The First Industrial Revolution turned the hand-tool worker into a machine tender; automation will turn the machine tender into a supervisor of an automatically controlled operating system.

> Basic to this new technology is the concept of feedback control or automatic self-correction. . . . Extend the concept of the furnace thermostat to industrial operations and you have an idea of automation. The worker does not operate the machine; he sets the level and repairs the system in case of a breakdown.[4]

In the foregoing chapter it was stated that one of the most easily observable and significant trends in American life is toward bigness: bigger government, bigger business, bigger unionism. The automatic factory, the electronic office device, the building of atomic power plants will tend to change the giant into the mammoth, if only on the basis of cost. It currently costs about $60,-000,000 to build an atomic reactor, and it costs a great deal of money to automatize a factory. It is not likely that any but the largest corporative units will be able to bear the cost of automation or the building of atomic reactors. And not only is automation expensive; *it is practical only on a large scale*—a further indication that widespread use of automation will give the giant corporations a new lever by which to squeeze out their smaller competitors. Meanwhile, the giants themselves will tend to centralize from within. Automatized forms of bookkeeping, communication, and computing will eventually make it possible for all—or most—administrative functions to be performed in one central office; whereas up to now the giant industries have operated from a number of geographically spread-out branch and subsidiary offices.

Widespread automation then, may very well destroy competition, and competition is one of the key concepts of the capitalist working under "natural economic laws." Competition is "good" in most capitalist theories because it is based on the idea that the good material which is most efficiently distributed will eventually drive out the bad material, less efficiently distributed, and that the law of supply and demand will in the long run prove more practical than any governmental planning apparatus.

The laws of supply and demand, however, do not work that way in a system in which big corporations become bigger and small businesses get squeezed out. These "laws" have not worked that way for a long time in our society. Nat Weinberg, Director of the Research and Engineering Department of the Congress of Industrial Organizations, points out the discrepancy between demand and distribution:

> Even a few management spokesmen are beginning to hint uneasily that something more may be needed than incantations to "natural economic forces" that "in the long run" will protect us against the horrors of mass technological unemployment.
>
> Madison Avenue and high-pressure techniques cannot make profitable customers out of underpaid or disemployed workers. . . . Periodically the ability of the economy to produce outruns the ability of the market to distribute. . . . The problem is clearly one of distribution, because the unmet needs of millions of American families, plus enormous national deficits in schools, hospitals, highways, resource developments, etc., plus the vast accumulation of needs of hundreds of millions outside our borders whose living standards are incredibly low, are sufficient to keep all our people, and all our machines, no matter how advanced, working at full capacity for many years, if not decades, to come.[5]

Weinberg reflects the prevailing contradiction among the *mixed economy* thinkers in the Congress of Industrial Organizations, who, on the one hand, realize that the problem is indeed one of distribution; and who, on the other hand, are more terrified of the "horrors of mass technological unemployment" than of the horrors of atomic warfare. CIO spokesmen are willing to defend the continuance of the armaments race in order to keep their members busy making the arms, continuing the race, and remaining employed.

In one sense, Mr. Weinberg and LIFE Magazine (representing two points of view which are usually found on opposite sides of the question) are in this case caught in a basic agreement. In an editorial for January 17, 1955, LIFE writers tell us about automation:

A whole new industry, now of three billion dollar proportions, has arisen *out* of automation. With a total of 2.7 million *not* working, we have been able to turn out and consume virtually as much goods as at the record heights of the boom. What this indicated is that the U. S. may be able to produce and consume at boom-levels yet still have a "permanent reserve" of unemployment which may increase. . . . Government recently has largely confined its recession-antidote public works projects to blueprinting the possibilities. Now it ought to draw a line—perhaps the present line of 2.7 million—above which unemployment will not be allowed to go without putting some of these projects into concrete. Fortunately, nearly all such measures can be made in capital improvements—new highways, schools, better housing, etc.—which will eventually pay for themselves by what they add to the income and brainpower of the economy. Since most of it ought to be done anyway, doing it now will keep us busy enough to defer the problems of greater leisure.[6]

In this way, both Nat Weinberg, speaking for the CIO, and LIFE Magazine (representing, in one way or another, management) agree on a plainly New Dealish solution to the bellyaches and consternations of the Second Industrial Revolution: build more expressways, raise wages and cut hours, look into unemployment insurance for those 2.7 million. These public-works enthusiasts almost always neglect to mention the fact that it was not the building of expressways which pulled us out of the Depression of the 1930's, nor yet the efforts to solve the housing problems of "one-third of a nation," but rather, the armaments program which preceded the Second World War.

What the holders of the "build expressways" viewpoint also neglect to mention is that so far no economy— mixed, capitalist, democratic or otherwise—has greatly changed the distributive system since the first Phoenician traders set out to sell their goods for the highest prices along the Mediterranean sea. Thinking men of the 1930's understood that something was a bit awry with the distributive system; it was an obvious fact at a time when, although people all over the world lacked food and shelter, coffee was dumped off the docks of

Brazil and cotton burned on the Gulf Coast in order that prices be kept high.

The First Industrial Revolution, now fading into the Second, has not at any time made the poor richer or the rich poorer. Money has changed hands, certainly, and rich men have gone bankrupt in this country while poor boys have become bank presidents, but this is not the same thing. The fabled American spirit of optimism and belief in progress seems to rest mainly on the idea that money can change hands more rapidly here than elsewhere, not on any hope that there will be an actual redistribution of income. In Spain, where national lotteries are legal and well attended, people also believe that they can get rich quick.

American Wealth and American Conscience

Although the problems of industrialism are common to countries other than the United States, it is the U.S. which has "had" industrialism worst. The United States, with six per cent of the world's population, produces just about 50 per cent of the world's industrial output, a fact which, as Stuart Chase says, "emphasizes the desperate poverty of millions of Asians and Africans. It tends to make Americans too cocky and their neighbors too envious, and skews not only the economy, but human relations." Nat Weinberg puts it in more economic terms: "the vast accumulation of needs of hundreds of millions outside our borders. . . ." How could both economics and human relations be set more aright? Chase answers: through the application of moral ballast, by cutting the Asians and Africans in on things, by creating a sane system of distribution on a planetary scale.

In an essay on Rudyard Kipling, George Orwell puts the matter to us:

> All left-wing parties in the highly industrialized countries are at bottom a sham, because they make it their business to fight against something which they do not really wish to destroy. They have internationalist aims, and at the same time they struggle to keep up a standard of life with which those aims are incompatible. We all live by robbing Asiatic coolies, and those of us who are "enlightened" all maintain that those coolies ought to be set free; but our standard of living and hence our "enlightenment" demands that the robbery shall continue. . . . He [Kipling] does not see that the map is painted red chiefly in order that the coolie may be exploited. . . . He sees clearly that men can only be highly civilized while other men, inevitably less civilized, are there to guard and feed them.[7]

Although all decent unionists must believe that people are more important than property, members of the American labor movement (like most Americans generally) feel that they must deny people in other areas of the world in order to give *their own* a fairly decent standard of living. The labor movement in this country, which today generally stands a little to the right of the late Franklin Delano Roosevelt, is crouched squarely on the horns of the moral dilemma which Orwell describes.

During World War II, the working-man made money, or at least more money than he had made for a long time before the war; there were many who resented this fact. Between the years 1941 and 1945 there were angry letters in the press to the effect that while workers made plutocratic wages in defense plants, the young men died overseas.

What was generally forgotten by the people who wrote those angry letters was the fact that management men and farmers and a number of other population groups were also making more money than they had before the war. Management, in particular, was making the kind of money which allowed its members to go to the best night-clubs, order ten-dollar meals, and support at least two homes, one in the suburbs, and one in the country during the summer months. The worker, on the other hand, was making enough money to put a down payment on a small home (very seldom in the suburbs), and maybe save for the inevitable rainy day or for the education of his children.

Generally the worker does not live that well. The worker may, as a matter of hard and cold fact, work his head off, save his money, plan for any number of rainy days, and still be caught in the maw of an unpredictable economy, as many laid-off workers in Detroit are caught today; or as miners in the eastern Kentucky coal fields were getting caught again in the late summer of 1954. (We began to see again the old familiar "depression" photographs from that area: the father, without prospect of work, the seven children in the three-room jerry-built cabin, need, hopelessness.)

The worker is always haunted by the fear of sudden poverty and layoffs and debt because no matter how well organized he is, no matter how hard he works, he is at the mercy of the upswings and downswings of an economy which nobody as yet has learned how to control.

And yet (and this "yet" is the other horn of the dilemma), the organized American worker lives generally at a level which, in comparison with most of the rest of the world, might very well be called "plutocratic." This is a sin which he shares with a great many of his fellow Americans. Working-men, too, shared in the blood money of the Korean war, even though many of them understood that it *was* blood money; working-men too, whether they like it or not, live to some extent off the naked and bowed backs of coolie labor in other parts of the world.

There are members of the American labor movement who feel guilty about this fact of life. (Probably more members of the labor movement feel guilty about it than do members of our business or propertied classes.) The American labor movement contributed thousands of dollars a year to the International Confederation of Trade Unions, which is responsible for sending money to trade union groups in Europe and Asia. The progressive elements in the American labor movement have for a long time been internationalist; they have passed resolutions supporting Point Four; resolutions repudiating the policy of "mass retaliation" which was thrown to the American public by the Eisenhower administration under the macabre title of "The New Look"; there are resolutions supporting projects in those ever-present *underdeveloped* areas of the world.

Nevertheless, the moral dilemma remains. Though many workers in this country would like to feel (in theory at least) that they support their working brothers in Europe, in South America, in Burma—they cannot, for actually they use wars to gain wage increases; they do so because they are inextricably part of the American economy and the American nationalism. There has never been a successful international working-men's movement opposing war. (The most sustained and enthusiastic attempt at such a movement, built under the auspices of the Socialists just before the First World War, collapsed miserably when the war broke out; the German leaders of that movement were brutally murdered.)

But at least working-class leaders have made the attempt at internationalism; the effort itself is more than many clergymen can boast of. German and English and American churches went promptly and rabidly nationalistic at the outbreak of World War I, and pastors all over the world prayed fervently and in public for God to get on their side. With some modifications—such as the forcible silencing of some Protestant portions of the German church—the same thing happened during the Second World War. Except for the pacifist fringes, there has not been in modern times any world-wide movement of churches opposing war.

Yet the Church, like the labor movement, is founded upon one ethical premise: the premise that people are more important than machines, and that the human soul has precedence over economics. And the American churches, like American unions, are caught upon the horns of the moral dilemma: they would stand, supposedly, for ethical values, and yet remain a living part of a rich America relentlessly preparing for war.

Automation—Paradise or Death?

Automation and the Second Industrial Revolution hold out the possibility of a paradise on earth for mankind— the fulfillment of the old dream of machines releasing humankind from drudgery.

At the same time, the mushroom over Hiroshima holds out the possibility of hell on earth—the fulfillment of the prophetic dream of an earth swallowed by fire.

Thus, at the very moment in human history when it is possible for us to commit race suicide through "vaporization," it is also possible for us to live in a kind of Utopia where "by the sweat of his brow" would come to mean "by the creative use of his leisure." There are perhaps few such immense ironies in all history.

The real irony lies in man's ambivalence to his possibilities. The ambivalence in itself is not new in history; it is only more acute. Between the mushroom over Hiroshima and the first Neanderthal man rubbing two sticks together and accidentally discovering fire, lies a long road of legendary ambivalence.

Many hundreds of years before Christ, when "the world" was still young, a legend of the martyr-hero, Prometheus, took form among men. Prometheus stole the knowledge of fire from the Gods in order to give it to mankind, and for his rebellion he was chained to a mountain in the Caucasus "where a vulture destroyed his liver . . . until Hercules set him free."

Although chained and, as it were, daily devoured, Prometheus remained heroic and defiant in the cause of Man, whose imagination he caught. Aeschylus wrote of him *(Prometheus Bound)* and Shelley, seeing his spirit in the French Revolution before it became the Terror, sanctified him as the leader of the resistance against the Powers That Be *(Prometheus Unbound)*.

Later eras came to regard the Promethean act as heroic, but the gift of fire as a not unmixed blessing. Henry Adams, fascinated by the Exposition of 1900 in Paris, contemplated the possibilities of the dynamo displayed there in much the same way that a thoughtful Neanderthal man might have considered the discovery of fire: with a troubled mind and a worried heart. As an historian, Adams was primarily interested in the contrast of the Age of Faith as against the Age of the Dynamo;

he was deeply influenced by Christian theology, which had changed the implications of the Promethean act. The Adam of the Christians had also decided to eat of the tree of knowledge, but unlike Prometheus, he sought to satisfy his curiosity rather than his desire for freedom; and Adam fell, not into proud resistance, but into the painful knowledge of good and evil, the reality of death, and the horror of self-awareness. Adam alienated himself from God through petty peek-sniffing rather than by an act of magnificent courage; and his spiritual descendant, Dr. Faustus, was obliged to sell his soul to the Devil in return for power, eternal youth, and the forbidden secrets of the Universe. Henry Adams saw the Paris Exposition as the Faustian will of Western man made concrete: here were on display the secrets already stolen or wrestled from a recalcitrant universe, and these displays were but powerful portents of things to come.

Henry Adams saw two great dramas running, like extended threads, down the center of Western civilization: in essence, the drama of Faust, and that of Christ. Adams refers to these two themes in his well-known juxtaposition of the Virgin Mother Mary of Chartres Cathedral and the Dynamo: the Age of Faith and the Age of Reason. One of the deepest implications of the Age of Faith was that man, like Faust, would bring on his own self-destruction if he pushed beyond the limits of the known world; that like Adam, he would unloose a new Pandora box of social-psychological ills, worse than those to which flesh is already proverbially heir.

The two world-views expressed themselves through varied doctrines: explorers and pioneers followed Prometheus and Faust; they charted new continents, made experiments, built the dynamo, harnessed the atom, constructed the revolutions. Eventually Christian theology accepted the existence of the dynamo, but always with reservations. Christ, like Prometheus, championed mankind; but whereas Prometheus offered men freedom and rebellion, Christ desired to give them reconciliation with God and the realization of love. This is why it is implicit in Christian theology that while the struggle with the gods of the sea and of darkness, of rain and of fire, goes on as in Promethean days, the deeper, darker, more terrifying struggle is within the heart of man. Within man, rage and love, anger and compassion fight for mastery; in rage men crucified Christ, and thereupon proceeded to adore him.

As the First Industrial Revolution progressed, it became evident that it was not the dynamo which was either good or evil, but the use to which it was put. The theme of humanity being devoured by the machine which it has created becomes a common one. E. M. Forster in *The Machine Stops* fantasies a world wherein men become as smooth and heartless as the Machine which governs them and which provides them with a religion (The Book of the Machine). Men grow hairless and passionless in a world of pure intellect created and serviced by the Machine. And in this world, Faustian man with his thousand seething aspirations is as outmoded as *Weltschmerz* man or Romantic Man.

In his novel *1984,* George Orwell foresaw an equally horrible human condition, but with fewer fantasy elements about it. H. G. Wells looked upon the machine with ambivalence: the dynamo could either save man from endless drudgery, or destroy man altogether, depending upon which way it was used. In a play of the 1920's, RUR, by Karel Capek, Rossum's Universal Robots are built by a group of scientists and sold all over the world to do the work of human beings; following constant improvement, the robots finally develop minds of their own, and there are so many of them that they unite and destroy humanity. Kapek chose a Christian answer to the dilemma; since the robots can do everything but reproduce themselves, the miraculous reappearance of heterosexual love among them opens the way to the development of a new human race from robot material.

As the Second Industrial Revolution follows hard upon the heels of the bomb over Hiroshima, and automation becomes an accomplished fact, the terrible paradox presses deep upon us. For the Faustian world is based upon the concept of the free flight of the individual through space—through space physical, mental, spiritual. It is because Christianity has set moral limitations to the universe that Faustian man has to make pact with the Devil in order to put aside those limitations in his flight toward omniscience.

The paradox arises in the fact that although—beginning with Renaissance man—the individual has been more technically free to explore the universe, his institutions, like his technology, have risen up bigger than life, as if to smother him. Bigger than life, bigger than the skyscrapers, and more crushing has this institutional-technological matrix become, so that it almost seems that the Forsterian-Adams kind of *gloomsayer* (as LIFE Magazine would name it) might be right. The dynamo, like the automatic factory, is amoral; and it has long since been seen that—Christian theology aside—man cannot live without moral ballast.

In its seeming lack of moral ballast, our modern world parallels that of the Roman Empire at the beginning or even in the height of its decline: the insane fury of our wars, the equally insane desire to pile up more money or power, the terrible effectiveness of modern tyranny. These things were also facets of an antique world which died many centuries ago. Even in dying, however, that world left us with the skin and bones of a culture which we sometimes love, sometimes hate, sometimes admire, perhaps envy, but which, above all, we cannot forget. The medieval world developed out of the dying body of classic civilization, just as the modern capitalist structure, in turn, grew out of a dying medieval heart. Christian values, as the people of the tenth or eleventh centuries conceived them, were antithetical not only to Faustian aspiration, but to the idea of capitalist aggrandizement and "progress." The Christian of the ninth century lived for rewards he could not see; earthly life was a testing ground where, at the best, a man might learn to practice ascetic self-denial. The mercantilist personality—solid, careful, accustomed to weighing both facts and money—had the effect of slowly dispelling the cloudy medieval world of demonic passion and tragedy. Do we wonder that the Willie Lomans of the modern world cannot face the existence of tragedy? It was Loman's spiritual forbears who were forced to fight through dark witch-infested woods to a straight road called "progress." When you are building a new structure of finance credit you cannot take time to search into the meaning of things. If the Christian of the Dark Ages had fixed his eyes inward too long, it was to become the besetting flaw of modern man to look for his salvation outside himself. And the decay of middle-class capitalist morality, when it came, was as catastrophic as the decay of medieval morality:

> It is probably true, as the Marxians would maintain, that decay came when the middle class no longer exercised its economic function—when it ceased, as in my generation, to be the group of active entrepreneurs and became a leisured class—but although this may have been the first cause of the phenomenon, it was powerfully aided by psychological influences . . . until it spread far beyond the limited number

of those who lived without work, affected poor and rich alike and even, so far as I was able to judge, made some superficial inroads upon the moral standards of the workers themselves. . . .

It was a general crumbling of middle-class morality throughout the West, starting in Paris (the logical center of Western taste) and reaching to the outposts of bourgeois culture. We can search the literature of the nineteenth century in all the Western countries in vain for an example of the kind of behavior on view in 1929 at any party in Paris, London, or New York. To our grandparents, the ordinary manners, conversation, conduct, and morals of educated and "respectable" people would have seemed suitable to the underworld.[8]

Capitalist ethics and capitalist economics had grown up along with the national state system. The kings of the struggling nationalist states had needed money, and the struggling merchants needed the protection of kings in order to carry on commerce. Bankers, indeed, might eventually rival kings, but the need of one for the other went too deeply for schisms to develop. The First World War displayed all the deep, fatal flaws in the nationalist state ordering of things. The effects of the War resulted in that moral breaking which Sheehan describes; like the people who survived the Black Plague of the fourteenth century, those who lived through the Great War were more inclined to worship at the shrine of Bacchus than at the tomb of Christ.

The Great War itself, however, was not the cause, but

rather the symptom of the disease. The disease lies at the heart of Western civilization, and a part of that disease is inherent in the tensions of nationalism, and another part in the inevitable flaws of capitalism.

> The important point to grasp here is that the capitalist super-ego was as much in conflict with man's diversified biological and social needs as that of the Christian Church: it was based on an equally wholesale system of denials and negations; and that fact is no less true, because capitalism denied another area of the human personality than that which the Church endeavored to subdue. . . .
>
> Decades and centuries must pass before the capitalist personality became supreme, before an entire civilization was ordered by its regular habits, stung by its acquisitiveness, lured by its promised comforts and luxuries, and debilitated by its automatisms. Before that state could be reached, the economic pattern of aggression needed reinforcement from the agents of government: their combined efforts were required to create the debased super-ego of the utilitarian man.[9]

It was not until the twentieth century that the agents of a New Deal government in the United States were to have a falling out with the capitalist "pattern of aggression"; it was not until the fight was on between the New Deal and some of the larger corporate structures that the idea of "government control" became associated in the popular mind with the death of "free enterprise." From the beginning of capitalism down into our own era it was usually taken for granted that the leaders of national

states would not merely be friendly—but protective—of
the growth of business.

> Nowhere in the seventeenth century was there any idea that
> public authority should pursue a hands-off policy in dealing
> with private property. . . . [In the Colonies] as in Eliza-
> bethan England, both town and central authorities inter-
> vened frequently in the economic life of the community, fix-
> ing wages and prices, regulating the quality of goods and
> the choice of occupations, and carrying on various com-
> munity enterprises. . . . At no time, in New England or the
> other regions, was there any prevailing idea that private
> property and public regulation were antagonistic concep-
> tions.[10]

It was only recently in the United States that democracy
—like nationalism—came to be associated as inextrica-
ble from capitalism. Nothing could be more erroneous.
Democracy, as we have seen, guarantees certain legal
and political rights to its people; and one of the most
profound ideas upon which democracy is based is that
human rights take precedence over property rights.
Equally erroneous is the propaganda device—used by
both Communists and Capitalists—that their particular
system of economics or government fits the needs of
"human nature." All government, and certainly all religious and cultural life in its institutional form is de-
signed to do just the opposite: to "conflict with man's
diversified biological and social needs," to suppress certain needs, and to channelize others which cannot be sup-

pressed, into directions beneficial to the state, the commonwealth, the ruling hierarchy, or to society as a whole. The early Christian Church strove to suppress the greed, pride, and lust inherent in "human nature" because it was greed, pride, and lust which made the early Dark Ages a jungle; capitalism strove to channelize greed, pride, and lust into economic areas.

> Those who fancy that this capitalist morality is a spontaneous and altogether natural one, founded on man's "real" nature, do not understand the amount of positive indoctrination, and effortful conversion that its eventual success demanded: the mere instinct of possessiveness, which a dog displays in the guarding of a bone or an infant in claiming a doll, had little to do with the unceasing preoccupation with arithmetical genius and the masterful acquisitiveness that motivated the capitalist.[11]

The dedicated Communist or Capitalist who argues that his particular system fits the "eternal verities" of human nature, argues from bias more than fact. Men have survived under precapitalistic and precommunistic structures. Men have adapted to feudalism, monogamy, polygamy, pantheism, cannibalism, dictatorship, democracy, oligarchy, monarchy, slavery, riches, poverty, paganism, Christianity, and even to industrialism and to hot war and cold peace. Creating or adapting to societal structures, men have changed them—and been changed by them. When they cannot adapt—when the Machine or the society or the government or the religion

twists their psychic joints into too many odd shapes—
they either change the institution that is twisting them,
or rise up and shatter the institution or the machine or
the state altogether.

Body and Soul

Go down to River Rouge in Detroit. River Rouge is just
a plain factory, of the First Industrial Revolution. It
has not thus far been automatized. And yet one's re-
action on surveying it may be as uniquely intense as
that of Henry Adams at the Paris Exhibition of 1900.
River Rouge is a world in itself; its hugeness goes
without saying; industrially, it is self-sufficient, with
its own steel mills, its own railroad tracks (99 miles
long). Thousands of men and women drive to that plant
during both the day and the night (for unless there is
a depression, the plant never rests); these men and
women drive to work in cars, their work consists of putting together car parts on the assembly lines, and when
they are through on their shift they drive home in cars.
The vastness and complexity of this system, as viewed
from the outside is overwhelming. There are tales of
engineers who would work twenty-four hours a day, if
need be, to keep the system in shape; their loyalty was
not to Ford, not to River Rouge, but to the Idea of the
system itself. You would think, looking at River Rouge,
that the men and women going in through the doors
existed only for the greater efficiency of the system.

A lot of men and women began to feel that way back in 1937. They were feeding the machine, all right, but the machine wasn't feeding them much in return except a cold mess of pottage. And people, being perverse, are usually prone to want more than they can get legally under any system. The robots didn't warm these people; the robots didn't give them spiritual comfort; nor did the robots hold forth with either love, nor its milder counterpart, the milk of human kindness. The Machine gave to the men who tended it only what was legally required—a mess of cold pottage.

So back in 1937, people up and kicked the Machine in the guts; they said, "We'll prove to you who's master here," and they sat down at the machines. Sure enough, the Machine stopped. The men who owned the machines yelled bloody murder; policemen marched in the streets of Flint and Detroit; strikers marched too, or just kept sitting on their haunches; the Governor was unhappy and the President was upset, but the Machine stopped. And the men didn't go back to work until they had assured themselves that they could stop the machine whenever they so desired.

Out of the strikes of 1937 and 1939, out of this perverse desire of men to be master of their own fate, came a new system in Detroit. Change that system—automatize the factories—and there will be another kind of system. Changes that you can see, and that the Detroit worker can feel. Because the social system has a deep effect upon us; the shape of the machine and the drudgery of labor without machines are real things; they are as real as those inner urges which make us curious to create machines in the first place.

But here is more recent history. During the summer of 1954, the Press Metals Company of Marysville, Michigan, decided to liquidate its assets, that is, go out of business. An official of the company was delegated to talk to the members of the CIO union in the plant concerning the liquidation. The Michigan CIO Council happened to take this man's speech down on tape.

The company official could hardly control the glee in his voice as he announced that the company would liquidate not only its assets, but the jobs of workers along with those assets. It's because of you guys, the official said in effect, that we're going out of business. You've got too many old men puttering around the shop, and you make us keep them on because they've got high seniority. You've given us too much trouble; why, every time one of your guys wakes up on the wrong side of the bed, you gotta strike! Well, this is it, boys. We're pulling out, and leaving you high and dry because this company is responsible to its stockholders and not to you!

Later, in a meeting held during one of the last weeks in July, union members were faced with a mean dilemma. They could accept company terms which, in effect, would eliminate the union altogether, with the promise that if they did so, the company would stay open a while longer, thus easing the layoff period, and giving the workers more time to find other jobs. The alternative open to the workers was to refuse company proposals, get laid off immediately, and suffer company reprisals which could consist of unfavorable publicity in state and local newspapers to the effect that "it was the irresponsibility of the union which caused Press Metals to go out of business."

Following heavy debate, members voted to reject company proposals, to retain their union membership, and to take the consequences of this action.

The Press Metals situation illustrates the heart of the moral issue which is at stake in any discussion of the trade union movement, or of the rights of men as against property rights. The heart of the situation is this: the workers at Press Metals did not own their jobs; rather, the "job," or the employer who gave them the job, *owned them* in the financial sense until such time as (1) the individual workers could leave the company to find better jobs; (2) the company itself would dismiss the workers because "the job" didn't need them any longer.

Although the company official who spoke so bitterly to the Marysville workers may certainly have been talking out of turn, he truthfully represented a fairly large and powerful segment of American management when he emphasized that the company's first and primary obligation was to its stockholders, *and not to the work-*

ers whom it might temporarily employ. In other words, the workers were—at all times and under any conditions —expendable.

The company official represented also (and more basically, perhaps, than he knew) the kind of hostility which exists between the worker in the shop and the foreman or industrial official or time-study man who is delegated to supervise the worker. We say basically because the dynamics of this mutual dislike exist beyond and outside the structure of either company policy or union policy. It is a personal thing which has only indirect relationship to union obligations or job duties; it is rooted in the resentment of individual workers who know that—except for certain union guarantees—they can be hired and fired at will. It is rooted further in the resentment of supervisors who come heartily to dislike the fact that they must, by the nature of things, deal with human inertia and individuality rather than with machines.

The voice of the Press Metals official betrayed the fact that he disliked to consider that actual human beings are full of unique little quirks; and when a human being breaks down, you can't just junk him as you can a machine, failing efforts to repair him. (You *can* junk him, of course, but with more trouble, and quite often public opinion is against it.) The company official could not help but consider workers to be lazy or indifferent people who, except for the threat of starvation, would refuse to work at all. On the other hand, the worker knows that no matter how affable some foremen may be (and certainly there are many in this era of "industrial psychology" who bring tact and even human warmth to the task of supervision, his basic job is still to get work out of people, just as the job of the company time-study man is to get *speed-up* work out of the people on whom he holds the watch.

These unique little quirks which mark human beings off from machines come out in varied ways. Werner Bloomberg, a social scientist from the University of Chicago, who has spent much time working in various factories, observes that even for the dullest and most repetitive tasks of the assembly line, workers create variety by what they call *tricks*, "particular ways of moving, of applying leverage, of swinging the arm or snapping the wrist." Workers were also prone to develop the machines into "personalities," attributing to them human willfulness and idiosyncracy. Although he does not minimize the monotony and uncreative character of many modern factory jobs, Bloomberg points out that "no technology can subvert or destroy the essential human-ness of the person—only other people can do that."

> Nowhere else have I felt as much freedom as I felt in the factory to be "myself" as a member of an ethnic tradition, as a person with a kind of temperament and disposition and a particular set of interests, as a personality with ups and

downs in how I felt about myself and others. Generally speaking, my fellow workers asked only that I learn to do my job well and that I stick with the group in its various conflicts with management. . . . Who in our society, I've had to ask myself, most clearly display a deep devotion to punctuality, lead routinized and rigidly repetitive lives, often seem as compulsive in their place as in their work? Not the workers I've known, but rather, the representatives of the more Puritanical elements of the middle classes.[12]

Today it is quite fashionable in some academic—and perhaps in quite a few church—circles to put a great deal of emphasis on the "friendly rapport" idea of union-management relations. It is believed in such circles that amiable smiles and goodwill on both sides will solve almost any dispute which might arise. After all, runs this theory, labor and management have everything in common. They both want to see the factories kept running and jobs plentiful and goods being produced; there is no reason that they cannot solve their grievances and get together to work for the common goal.

It is precisely the conflict between "the more Puritanical elements of the middle classes" and the descendants of the "feudal craftsmen or peasants who were inducted into the industrial army and brought many of their cultural patterns with them," which the "friendly rapport" theorists overlook. They overlook, too, the hard actuality that no amount of friendly shoulder patting has been able to solve the worker-foreman antagonism of which we have already spoken. The *glory* of hard work (this idea which is still so intimately associated with the Protestant ethic) simply does not exist for the factory worker, who is harnessed to an intensely routinized industrial process, and to *the tending of someone else's machine.* (And, as everyone knows, the large chain stores, the huge consolidated farm, and the corporation have muscled further and further into the territory which once belonged to the small independent businessman or the family farm.)

Now it is obvious that both management and labor want to keep the factories running, the goods flowing, and the jobs plentiful—but they want to accomplish these things for radically different purposes. It is true that when Charles Wilson of General Motors states that "what is good for General Motors is good for the country," and when the CIO says that "the worker should not have to pay for the failure of the employer to produce," they would seem to stand on the same moral grounds. General Motors is morally and economically good as long as it produces; General Motors is morally and economically bad when it fails to produce, when workers get laid off, when consumers can't buy. (If anything distinguishes American culture, it is the feeling which runs through it that the elusive thing called *happiness* is somehow associated with productive capacity, and that those who cannot attain happiness or production in America have something wrong with them.)

Both management and labor, then, would seem to be

frightened to death of *idleness*. But management is frightened because it believes men to be anarchists at heart; it believes that you can't get a man to work at all unless you threaten him with starvation. Meanwhile, unions are frightened of idleness because the word itself brings up visions of mills shutting down, soup lines, apple carts, and the old song: "Why don't you work like other people do? How can I work when there's no work to do?"

It is just at this point that the economic question becomes indistinguishable from the moral one. The Guaranteed Annual Wage Plan (finally agreed upon in modified form by both the automobile workers and a good part of the automobile industry as well) is based on the theory that management, like every other section of society, has obligations as well as rights. Technically, the UAW is presenting a plan which would guarantee the worker against short work-weeks and long weeks of layoff. (The Guaranteed Wage is referred to frequently as the Full Employment Plan.) But the moral implication of the plan is clear: a company should not be allowed to take up and leave, go out of business, or lay off workers at will (as in Marysville); a company owes consideration to the workers whom it employs, the community in which it is located, and the economy of which it is a part and from which it, too, draws sustenance. In other words, if management is allowed to be irresponsible, it will eventually strangle the goose which lays the golden egg. (And in CIO theory the goose that lays the golden egg is not management, but a healthy consumer economy.)

Labor in this instance stands upon the principle that because food is a universal need, there is a universal morality demanding the fulfillment of that need. This, one might add, is a unique thing—unique, and indigenously American. No prenineteenth century society (with the possible exception of the brief-lived tribunals of the French Revolution) ever conceived of such a moral obligation. Very few twentieth century societies have spelled out the obligation so concretely. Yet, in actuality, the idea is a Christian one, for essentially American labor is demanding that the maxim, "Thou art thy brother's keeper," be applied on specifically economic grounds, "Thou art the keeper of thy workers." The outline of the Guaranteed Annual Wage plan implies, it seems, a double edge to the maxim: ". . . as thy workers are the keepers of thee."

Behind demands for better wages, for shorter working hours, for pensions, for the elimination of child labor, for the Guaranteed Annual Wage, stands one deep and passionate desire: *the desire of individual workers to be treated as human beings rather than as commodities on the market*. Just as the genius of Protestantism has always been the demand that the individual conscience be held in respect, so the true aim of any bona fide labor union is that the individual be held in respect, and that the uses of the industrial system be prevented from swallowing him up as if he were a piece of timber or a slab of steel. (This, incidentally, is the reason that the British lay ministry had such a profound influence on the British trade union movement. In America, where there is far less contact between Protestantism and labor, both groups have suffered from the lack of rapport, a lack which, again, has been caused by the turning of Protestantism toward middle-class values.)

The Answer of Religion

The Protestant left wing is much nearer in its ethical outlook to the social goals of the working-class movement, for left-wing Protestantism, unlike Puritanism, is a synthesis of the rationalistic and the Christian. "The left wing," says Roland Bainton, "is composed of those who separated church and state and rejected the civil arm in matters of religion." If the autonomy of the individual in matters of religion is accepted, then the autonomy of the individual in political and secular affairs must also be recognized. This concern for individual moral perfection means, among other things, that the individual is more important than the wealthiest corporation or the most efficient automatic factory. His institutions are for his use; he is not for the use of the institution. Society, for the left-wing Protestant, is always under examination and re-examination; society is always subject to the possibility of improvement—an improvement either radical or gradual. Left-wing Protestant theory is based upon the idea that individuals, through the radical freedom of the self, must make choices, and must take the consequences of those choices. This means that individuals can act sincerely within the church only in terms of their faith; it means that the church itself will, if it is to be effective, remain always in tension with the wider society.

As things—both economic and political—become every day, in every way, bigger and bigger, the outlook for the individual becomes, in many areas, dimmer and dimmer. Institutional frameworks of great size tend to do great harm to the individual psyche simply through the fact of intense impersonality. Man, the individual, still lives in a highly personalized world; he lives with the love and hate, the compassion and anger, the rage and pity, of the pre-Promethean. Man, the sociological animal, still lives within and gains warmth from small primary groups, familial ties, community frameworks, a circle of friends. His political structure remains archaic and, on a global scale, anarchistic. The possibly fatal irony of this predicament is illustrated in a headline from *The Los Angeles Times* for January 23, 1955: "TRIP TO MOON HELD POSSIBLE BY 1965. Delay May Be Caused, However, by Concentration on War Weapons."

Man, the ethical being, is still a creature who finds it

impossible to live without moral limitations. Reinhold Niebuhr states the oldest of theological reasons for distrusting not only Faust, but what he defines as "modern Socratic culture":

> Much evil is undoubtedly done in sheer stupidity, but the basic human problem is the constant expression of the self's pride, will-to-power, and avarice. Bertrand Russell defines the basic human inclination as the desire for "power and glory." This is probably as good a definition of sin as any . . . which any thoughtful observer must recognize as being more illuminating about man, particularly man in his contemporary setting than all the Socratic interpretations which try to derive virtue from intelligence.
>
> The modern "Socratic" culture . . . even if it acknowledged the reality and the "dignity" of human selfhood . . . never came to terms with the "misery" of man. Briefly, that "misery" is man's inclination to use his freedom not as the instrument of virtue, but as a tool of self-glorification, and consequently as an instrument of social strife and injustice.[13]

The conquest of the moon may be near; the conquest of man's inner misery is evidently not near. Yes, said E. M. Forster in considering this question, the struggle is within the soul of man, but there can be seen no "change of heart" bursting upon us in the sudden future. If love and curiosity build the world, pain and hate destroy it. All great religious movements have been built upon the control of rage and pain for a larger purpose; all great religious movements have implied also that the change of heart, the leap of faith, can happen. Experience tells us that it does happen—but to individuals. Masses of men may take up, at any given time, enthusiasm for some cause; it is usually only individuals who are able to cast out fear through love.

Following this thought further—into the political sphere—it would seem obvious that if something is wrong with the distributive system, then that system should be changed. This does not mean that it will be changed, but only that it can be changed, and needs changing. Like E. M. Forster, we cannot go along with the Change of Heart boys; nor can we see much hope that the "Use Your Head" rationalists will effect, in the near future, a beautiful, well-planned House of Man. Christian socialism would probably provide some of the answers for both skewed human relations and wacky economics, but any real possibilities of such an answer or series of answers being put into effect soon seem doubtful.

There is always a middle ground of thought. The rationalist, thinking out what he blandly terms "foreign affairs" would say that "we must learn to co-exist with Russia, because in a shooting war neither of us would be the gainer; a shooting war may destroy us all, and who is the gainer then?" The Christian, on the other hand, would say that co-existence is nonsense; only strong love is equal to strong hate; only an intense adherence to the moral law can save us now. The middle ground might be called the "muddle through" men, those who hold the view that somehow, in some way, the human race sort of just goes on surviving by the skin of its teeth. The "muddle through" school recognizes that the variety and range of special interest, peculiar antagonisms, intense phobias, makes it difficult for a rational planner to begin to implement logical plans about distribution or democracy; they understand also that although co-existence for the sake of survival makes a strong claim upon human beings, it is countered by other claims just as strong. Men will fight bloody and profitless wars or spend their time thinking up ways of gaining political power which they do not need; and these things are done with the greatest disregard of reason; sometimes they are done with little sense of survival, against "self-interest." A great deal of evil, as Niebuhr says, is done out of sheer stupidity; a great deal of evil is also done out of simple perversity and emotional imbalance.

Those whose pride in being human is often outraged by the "muddle through" boys, would want to believe, in their heart of hearts, that we are more heroic than this. But there can be little doubt that man's perversity is both his salvation and his undoing. So perverse indeed that he makes a hero out of Prometheus, the image of pride and defiance; and a God out of Christ, the image of humility and love.

Chapter 3

At night, on the third floor of the palace, guarded by eighty sentinels, who every quarter of an hour cry aloud a whole sentence, Ernest IV trembles in his room. . . . If a plank creaks in the floor, he snatches up his pistols and imagines that there is a Liberal hiding under his bed. . . . Absolute power has this advantage, that it sanctifies everything in the eyes of the public: what harm can there be in a thing that nobody notices? Our policy for the next twenty years is going to consist in fear of the Jacobins.[1]

—HENRI BEYLE (STENDHAL)

Government by Law
and Government by Men

THERE is ample evidence that in the 1950's and '60's the American policy will be based on fear of the Communists. Have the investigating committees for loyalty been confused on what constitutes conspiracy against the government? Can we set ourselves straight on what a man owes society and what society owes the individual? The whole history of democracy since its birth over three hundred years ago has recorded example after example of the intolerance of those who preached toleration. One great contrast between American ideology and American practice reveals itself in race relations. The uniqueness of the American constitution roots in its concept of liberty under law, and yet the enforcement of the right to liberty is one of the most difficult of all governmental problems. Kermit Eby's subpoena, the South Deering dilemma, and the Sacco-Vanzetti case described in this chapter are illustrations of that fact.

I Receive a Subpoena[2]

I had heard, sometime in the early 1950's, that American policy for the next twenty years was going to consist in fear of the Communists. My chance to test that premise personally came on a humid Wednesday afternoon during the summer of 1953, when a man appeared in my office and laid before me a long piece of paper, a subpoena to appear before the Jenner subcommittee of the Internal Committee of the Judiciary of the United States.

Since it was the first subpoena that I had ever received, I wondered for a moment what crime it was that I had committed. Then colleagues and students, friends and well-wishers, began to come in to congratulate me. "We are so glad it happened," they said. "You will speak for us. You will take up our cause."

I had the odd suspicion that perhaps some of their congratulatory zeal derived from the fact that I had been subpoenaed and not they.

I myself was not so overjoyed. Jenner had announced that the hearings were secret in order to "protect" those on trial, which meant, of course, that speculation would run wild. One newspaper reporter called me and said, "I *assume* you got a subpoena?" The *Chicago Sun Times* observed (shrewdly enough) that an "invitation to appear before the committee casts doubt on a man's reputation." Yes, indeed—any man's reputation. The reputation of the purest—or the most harmless—man.

It soon became apparent that Senators Jenner and Butler were not out to judge a specific criminal act, but the degree of political evil in me. By what standard of political purity they could judge me, and what they might do to me if they found me not up to par, I could not tell, so I tried to find out. A law student subpoenaed that summer along with me also spent some time trying to find out. It seemed that no one really knew much about either the powers or the prerogatives of the committee. For all practical purposes, the committee seemed to function in the same way as the Inquisition in Spain: the clerical arm (the Jenner Committee) hands over the victim, following interrogation, to the secular arm (in this case my employer, the University of Chicago). The secular arm is responsible for active punishment (in this case, firing the man, and then making it difficult for him to earn a living elsewhere). Of course, if the secular arm doesn't come through—and in this case the University stood firm behind its teachers—the whole system collapses.

In the end, I told Senator Jenner (who comes from my home state of Indiana), what to me was obvious: that I had never been and was not now (nor, I suppose, intending to become) a Communist; that I had always, by virtue of long-held conviction, been anti-authoritarian; that I belonged to the order of the Brethren by birth and was both a minister and a professor by trade. Further, I intimated that if they were to try me, they would have to try the entire Protestant heritage of which I was a part. With various apologies, the Committee then informed me that they had not been aware of these things, and instructed me, after some hesitation, to return to my home.

It was about this time that I began to feel a little angry. Having been denied a public hearing, I learned later (and from the newspapers) that Professors Ernest Burgess and Anton J. Carlson, and myself, had been asked to give testimony because we had "been keeping bad company." It appeared, then, that it was not we who were interesting in ourselves, but rather, the degree of political evil in our possible associates.

Since I had been given little or no time to express myself on the matter, I began to feel decidedly balked. I would have told the Committee (had they asked me) that I consider the company I keep to be my own business. I have friends who belong to the National Association of Manufacturers; I also have friends in the "red unions" which seceded from or were kicked out of the CIO. To choose one's associates for their intrinsic interest rather than their possible influence or connections would seem the least a man might offer toward the ideal of serious and civilized living. I would also have told the Jenner Committee (had they asked me), that I have undoubtedly gone to meetings where Communists were present; perhaps I have even appeared on a couple of letterheads with Communists. The horror of such associations I somehow don't recognize. It would seem that by the law of human averages, Communists, through contact with people like me from the *outside* world might every once in a while be tempted to change their affiliations. That growing legion of ex-Communists, some of whom insist on writing books on their conversion *out* of the party, might testify to this fact.

I began to feel balked, too, when I considered the position of some of my compatriots who had been called up by Velde or Jenner or Eastland, and who had pleaded the Fifth Amendment. They had in this way incurred the label, "Fifth Amendment Communist," (a McCarthy invention) which, in effect, reverses the due process of Anglo-Saxon law (hitherto interpreted to mean that a man is innocent until he is proved guilty). The Fifth Amendment had been incorporated into the Constitution in order to guard against the possibility of Star Chamber proceedings: the secret hearings, the arbitrary rulings behind closed doors, no chance to face your accusers, men forced to testify against themselves. In actual practice, the Fifth Amendment has been invoked quite often, not in self-protection, but from fear of being forced into the unenviable role of the informer. Once having answered the first question (Are you now or have you ever been a Communist?), a witness is forced, on pain of contempt of court, to answer all following questions. Most non-Communists who *got around* politically in the 30's had friends or acquaintances or enemies who were admitted Communists. I was luckier or more wicked than some of my colleagues in this respect: it happened that my contacts with "subversives" did not include self-confessed Communists; I was not in the habit of asking social or professional connections their political slant. Had I *known*, however, I might have taken recourse to the Fifth Amendment. Someone should inform those inquisitors who are of an almost ridiculously literal temperament that men of honor are nowhere reassured by this talk of "vast and horrible conspiracy." Such talk only generates the deceptive idea that a witness's plain duty is to set aside all simple human decency and to start naming names whenever he can think of names to name to a committee which laps it all up with a tape recorder.

What Is "Conspiracy"?

At this point in my argument, someone always jumps up with a question, which generally goes like this: "But wouldn't you be willing to inform in court on a man whom you saw commit a murder, even if he were your friend? And if so, why wouldn't you bear witness against a man who, as a Communist, was part of a deadly conspiracy against the United States government?" Along with this question usually goes the accusation: that I, and men like me, are "soft-minded." I shall probably be warned that Sparta won out over Athens because Sparta had the tougher, bigger battalions, and meanwhile—as everyone knows—Athens was getting "soft," that is, civilized, and of course that is why the Athenians lost.

The answer to that particular question comes, I think, in two parts. There is all the difference in the world between testifying in a criminal court, and in a court whose real function is to test the conformity of a man's political opinions. Jenner, Velde, and McCarthy have not, to my knowledge, produced for trial one man engaged in conspiracy, sabotage, or murder. (In the Rosenberg case, which was not the affair of a Congressional Investigating Committee at all, two persons were convicted of giving atomic secrets to Russia. Alger Hiss was sent to jail on charges of perjury.) In addition, the numerous Un-American Activities Committees have dredged up a certain number of ex-Communists here and there over the country. A good many of these ex-Communists were honest men, who joined the Party because they were convinced that it was right, and who left it because they had become convinced that it was not right. They were not accused of giving away atomic secrets, committing sabotage, or murdering people in back alleys. Further, the committees have produced a great number of men like myself and my colleague, Anton J. Carlson, at the University of Chicago. I was sent home in the way that I have described. Mr. Carlson (a famed biologist and a man of fine, conservative temperament) was accused of having sponsored a Young Communist Club on campus for a period of time. He ad-

mitted to this charge readily enough, and said that he
had consented to act as sponsor of the club because, although he did not agree with its members, he did, like
Voltaire, agree with their right to disagree. Mr. Carlson
was also sent home, after some confusion on the part
of the judges.

The first part of my answer, then, is the statement that
the Un-American Activities Committees which have been
touring the country in our time, are not engaged in the
investigation of criminal acts of violence (like the La-
Follette or Kefauver committees, which had legitimate
concerns with which to deal). Rather, the "Un-Ameri-
cans" are political groups engaged upon political ends.

Render unto Caesar

The second part of Kermit Eby's answer takes longer,
and is more difficult. It has to do with questions such as
these: What belongs rightfully to Caesar and what to
God? What does a man owe society and what does
society owe the individual? The complexities of these
questions go a long way back. Caesar is a persistent
figure in human history, and the tendency to give him
more and more room is an insistent temptation even for
men who are convinced that the moral law is everywhere
and anywhere superior to the flexible laws of men (even
during those frequent periods when one emergency follows another, and we are always being advised to set
aside moral law in order to extricate ourselves from one

more emergency). Socrates, having considered these questions thoroughly, answered them ironically and personally: the State had the right (that is, the power) to kill him; but, by the same token, he had the right to continue holding opinions regardless of their unpopularity with the State.

The tendency to give unto Caesar even more than Caesar asks is a very great temptation; it appears under the most approved labels: love of country, duty, honor, the desire to serve a cause Larger than Oneself, the desire to be solid with the Many under a ready-made morality and an easily understood flag. The common endeavor of war, unlike the common but mundane endeavor of paying taxes, is fraught with the possibility of solidarity and heroic action. It was not so long ago that men of the Western world were hung, drawn, and quartered, garotted, or burned at the stake for their religious and/or political opinions. The wars we Westerners now wage are in the name of national states; Protestants no longer fight Catholics on the fields of Germany, but "God" becomes confused with "Country" all the same. Nowadays it is more tribal—the God of the Russians against the God of the Americans rather than one religious idea against another.

We in America have come to consider it generally barbaric to kill men for their political or religious opinions. (Somebody did suggest recently, that there should be a death penalty for Communists, but this measure is still considered too excessive to be incorporated into law.) We in America also boast that we have no political prisoners. (This is not strictly true; it is simply that we bunch all our prisoners—including conscientious objectors and Jehovah's Witnesses and framed politicals—into the same general area as safe crackers and arsonists. The Spanish-speaking peoples, who are more honest about some things, have, as a matter of course, a strict dividing line between their politicals and their criminals.)

Still and all, the general American sentiment is against hanging men for what, with delicate nuance, we call "their convictions." We consider it uncivilized. We have always held ourselves just a little above the people in the rest of the world. We have a superior system of law, you see, and a superior system of government, not to mention our superior standard of living. Ergo, our logic runs, we are a superior set of people.

We often neglect to remember that the basic facts of human life—and of politics—are pretty much the same everywhere. Just as in Germany, given the proper conditions, something deep in men responded to Hitler, so here, something in the human grain responds to McCarthy. The inquisitorial mind is as likely to be hatched in Main Street, U.S.A., as in Seville or Moscow.

The Nature of Martyrdom

Again, our comparatively successful experience with

democracy has made many of us Americans forget the hard facts of politics. (Especially do we Protestants tend to forget how intensely political our immediate spiritual forebears got to be, and how many of them seemed to end up hanged, drawn, and quartered.) Because of our national birth in revolution, we are taught in grammar school to revere the martyr. We are also taught (more by implication than by fact) that if a cause is righteous it is bound to win out. "The blood of the martyrs is the seed of the Church." But by and large we learn about those dissident groups which happened to be successful; thus we are prone to overlook the fact that the great majority of those who revolt against duly constituted authority are not successful. The great liberal spokesman, John Stuart Mill, reminded us of this fact in the nineteenth century:

> History teems with instances of truth put down by persecution. If not suppressed forever, it may be thrown back for centuries. To speak only of religious opinions: the Reformation broke out at least twenty times before Luther, and was put down. Arnold of Brescia was put down. Fra Dolcino was put down. Savonarola was put down. The Albigeois were put down. The Vaudois were put down. The Lollards were put down. The Hussites were put down. Even after the era of Luther, wherever persecution was persisted in, it was successful. In Spain, Italy, Flanders, the Austrian Empire, Protestantism was rooted out: and most likely would have been so in England, had Queen Mary lived, or Queen Elizabeth died. *Persecution has always succeeded, save where the he-*

retics were too strong a party to be effectually persecuted.
Men are not more zealous for truth than they often are for
error, and a sufficient application of legal or social penal-
ties will generally succeed in stopping the propagation of
either.[3]

And George Orwell, who in the twentieth century was
perhaps as great a spokesman for liberalism as Mill in
the nineteenth, gives us an even grimmer picture:

We in England . . . nourished for hundreds of years on a
literature in which Right invariably triumphs in the last
chapter . . . believe half instinctively that evil always defeats itself in the long run . . . in our mystical way we feel
that a régime founded on slavery *must* collapse. But it is
worth comparing the duration of the slave empires of antiquity with that of any modern state. Civilizations founded
on slavery have lasted for such periods as four thousand
years. . . . When I think of antiquity, the detail that
frightens me is that those hundreds of millions of slaves
on whose backs civilization rested generation after generation have left behind them no record whatsoever. We do not
even know their names. In the whole of Greek and Roman
history . . . I can think of only two, or possibly three. One
is Spartacus and the other is Epictetus. Also, in the Roman
room at the British Museum there is a glass jar with the
maker's name inscribed on the bottom, "Felix fecit. . . . "
But in fact he may not have been a slave; so there are only
two slaves whose names I definitely know, and probably few
people can remember more. The rest have gone down into
utter silence.[4]

Like the slaves, the vast majority of unsuccessful dissidents have gone down into silence, too. We remem-

ber only the names of those who were heavily enough *put down* to earn themselves a footnote-size bloody smear on the pages of a history book.

Now in actual practice, there are only two kinds of dissidents who are tolerated in any society: (1) those who, as Mill points out, are so strong that they cannot easily be hunted down and done away with; (2) those who are so weak as not to be threatening to constituted authority. In a really monolithic power structure, not even the second type can be tolerated very far for very long, for *no* human being, in such a society, can be permitted much variation. From what we know of modern-day Russia, even slight defections from official philosophy are punished rapidly. However, in any structure which can permit some variation, the man who goes out alone, preaching the integrity of the individual conscience, may be afforded toleration without too much strain on the part of the state. Many such individualists (such as, in American society, vegetarians, nudists, professors, prohibitionists, some types of conscientious objectors, poets, believers in free love, and so on) gain the reputation for being cranks, and their toleration is assured as long as very few people take them seriously.

It is a very different matter when the state presumes to be dealing with a matter of conspiracy, that is, a sect of powerful or potentially powerful dissidents bent on *acting out their beliefs*. The Puritans constituted such a conspiracy during the reign of Queen Elizabeth. For

several decades before the Revolution, Bolshevik leaders wrote, pamphleteered, organized, and conspired
from Siberia, a place to which they were at frequent
intervals, exiled. Likewise, there had been occasional
persecutions under Elizabeth of individual sectarians,
but these persecutions were mild in nature, as Siberia in
1897 was mild in comparison to Dachau. Elizabeth was
forced to tolerate even the more militant Puritan sects,
because they were too strong to be easily put down;
prerevolutionary Czars were in something of the same
position. And the Puritans, like the Old Bolsheviks,
gained time during their period of halfway suppression
to develop their "thought, propaganda, code, and full
complement of differences, inconsistencies, compromises, and extravagances such as revolutionary movements seem always the more likely to incur the longer
their consummation is delayed."[5]

Like all real revolutionaries, both the Puritans and
the Bolsheviks proposed to do away with an entire system of order: social, religious, institutional. The Elizabethan Order—a system which Shakespeare accepted as
good and true—consisted of a great Chain of Being,
with Heaven at the top of the chain, Hell at bottom, and
the earth balanced between. In this order, each man had
his place, just as heaven and hell had their place. This
was the Elizabethan universe; it was also the Elizabethan
social order, with the divine right of kings as an integral
part of the order of the universe. To upset that order was

to outrage nature, to cause chaos, to bring about disharmony in the very nature of things.

This, then, was the kind of conspiracy which the Puritans represented within the body politic—not just a change in the economic or social order; but a change in the universal system of things, an outrage, if you will, against the Divine Law. The impact of the success of these conspirators in gaining power, beheading Charles I, and setting in his place a commoner named Oliver Cromwell, was (even when we recollect it at a distance and in tranquillity), explosive.

The Birth of Democracy

And it was here, in the 1640's, in England, following the killing of a king and the further killing of thousands of nameless people in civil war, that the real structure of modern-day parliamentary procedure—as we in the English-speaking world know it—was given foundation. That foundation was built in the endless theological and political squabbles of the Westminster Assembly which, from 1643 to 1645 was haunted by the "red spectre of toleration," and dominated by the Presbyterians who had "but few roots, and but negligible lay following in England."[6]

The "red spectre" haunted the Assembly (as many years later Marx declared in the *Manifesto* that communism would haunt Europe) because the Puritans had yielded completely to the divisive influences always in-

herent in fanatic factionalism. They had split, and split
again, and none of them could really tolerate each other.
The dominating Presbyterians were generally regarded
as bigots (as most often those who dominate must be
bigots); the Presbyterians formed political alliances and
fought for power against Congregationalists, Baptists,
and Brownists.

Ranged against these competing powers in the Assembly were all the dissenting groups in England. These
included:

(1) Quakers (described as "eccentric and antisocial exhi-
    bitionists").

(2) Roman Catholics, of whom only one was reported to
    have been put to death under Cromwell's Common-
    wealth in England. However, in Ireland many died in
    battle; the Irish took up arms against the Common-
    wealth and the "duly constituted authority" thereof, and
    engaged in open civil war.

(3) Anglicans, members of the State Church of England
    brought into being by Henry VIII. The Presbyterian
    majority in Parliament was set dead against the An-
    glicans, although Cromwell himself was willing to ex-
    tend to them a large measure of administrative toler-
    ance, as long as they did not take part in Royalist plots
    (that is, start a conspiracy within the body politic of
    the Commonwealth).

(4) Socinians, with whom Cromwell dealt tolerantly and
    patiently.

(5) Jews. Cromwell would have admitted Jews to England
    as a stimulus to trade, but he was overruled by the ob-

jections of London merchants, who disliked the threat of Jewish competition. And London merchants were the economic foundation of the Commonwealth.

Oliver Cromwell who was, for any age, an extraordinary man, provided the balance which somehow, in some way, kept the sectarians from devouring each other, and from fighting new civil wars within civil war. Cromwell was a difficult and narrow man who hated art, music, the knotty questions of tolerance, of majority rule, of democratic procedure under law. It was Cromwell who did most to thwart the fixed Presbyterian desire to "establish a Puritan orthodoxy in England," although his policy of toleration was often enough roadblocked by the need to face "harsh political realities."[7] Cromwell was also outstanding as a successful heretic. We who have been reared in the concept of the triumph of Democracy and Right tend to glorify the dissident without, sometimes, realizing what he stands for. The heretic can, indeed, be an unpleasant person with whom to deal. And triumphant heretics often turn to intolerance as a matter of course. Calvin burned his own heretics at Geneva; once his rule was established, Luther permitted no disagreement within his Germanic provinces. We all know about the Bolsheviks. Savonarola (who indeed was *put down*) was a difficult and narrow man who hated art, music, literature, and all the trappings of civilization perhaps as much as he hated the double dealings of the rich and the immoralities of the clergy. His voice thunders down to us over the centuries like the harangue of a backwoods preacher as he brings down fire and brimstone on bad women, the drinkers of corn "likker," and those who participate in the fleshpots of urban cultural centers.

Savonarola, "a small frame racked and haunted with visions, frustrated aspirations, and introverted storms," facing the dying Lorenzo de Medici, was not merely a martyr, but a civilization wrecker. Lorenzo was the epitome of the sophisticated minority, a gentle libertine, a man of culture and manners, master of complex societal arrangement and subtle ideas, a man who bore the responsibilities of government seriously, and yet not without humor. The kind of relationship that Lorenzo would have with Savonarola was inevitable.

> Lorenzo was disturbed. His grandfather had founded and enriched the monastery of San Marco (where Savonarola preached); he himself had given to it lavishly; it seemed to him unreasonable that a friar who could know little of the difficulties of government, and who idealized a liberty that had been merely the right of the strong to use the weak through hindrance by law, should now undermine, from a Medici shrine, that public support upon which the political power of his family had been built. He tried to appease the friar; he went to Mass in San Marco's, and sent the convent rich gifts. Savonarola scorned them. . . . Lorenzo sent five leading citizens to argue with him that his inflammatory sermons would lead to useless violence, and were unsettling the order and peace of Florence; Savonarola answered by telling them to bid Lorenzo do penance for his sins. A Fran-

ciscan friar famous for eloquence was encouraged to preach
popular sermons with a view to drawing the Dominican's
audience away; the Franciscan failed. . . . The ailing Lorenzo made no further effort to interfere with his preaching.[8]

It was left for less civilized men than Lorenzo to put
Savonarola down—not because he represented the black-
and-white conviction of the backwoods, but because he
threatened their power, and therefore their self-interest.
There is a good deal of the backwoods—the simplicity of
great bitterness—in most reformers. Seldom is one found
who combines political sophistication with the intensity
of world-shaking conviction.

"Preach Back"

But such a combination was Oliver Cromwell. Believing
himself to be in direct contact with God, Cromwell felt
that, like him, all men should be forced to find God's
truth *in their own way*. And even though Cromwell was
brought to power in a theocratic state, he barred the
clergy from any real influence in government, since he
was not at all sure that the clergy was much closer to
God than he himself.

Cromwell's faith was completely unsympathetic and anti-
dogmatic. He was, so far as organized religion was concerned, a spiritual anarchist, who was willing to extend the
principle of private judgment and spiritual freedom to the
uttermost limits of the diversity included under the name of
Protestantism. . . . English sectarianism had, during the

Civil War, been crystallized into a formidable political and moral force and . . . was, under the pressure of Presbyterian bigotry, united only upon the principle of religious toleration. Sectarianism formed the shaft of the spear of which Cromwell was the head. . . . He came to believe that religious toleration was important, but after he had come to power the loose confederation of sects began to crumble, *and sectarianism itself began to manifest the intolerance of a dominant majority group.* . . . Cromwell sought to drive public opinion faster and farther than the slow and inarticulate instincts of the mass mind could follow. . . . Public opinion, though changed perceptibly and permanently under his tutelage, relapsed with the Restoration into a period of recuperation and stock-taking in the more traditional grooves of thought and policy.[9]

There is a delightful story told about Cromwell. When a group of Presbyterian clergymen came to him in 1656 to complain that the Anglican clerics were taking their congregations away from them, Cromwell asked, "After what manner do the cavaliers debauch your people?"

"By preaching."

"Then preach back again."[10]

The Anglicans evidently preached better, because "England entered the Civil Wars and emerged from the Interregnum predominantly Anglican, though sectarianism had made enormous and permanent gains."[11]

During this period of ferment, intellectuals and writers were neither silent—nor necessarily more tolerant—than other parts of the population. Jeremy Taylor, for

example, did not really like Cromwell's policy of toleration, for, said Taylor, "This is the way of peace rather
than truth. It is indeed a highly reasonable way. Yet
how can the intolerant, who seek not equality, but absolute rule, be themselves tolerated? Complete toleration
is better in contemplation than in practice . . . for divide
the church in twenty parts, and, in whatever part your
lot falls, you and your party are damned by the other
nineteen."[12]

More than three hundred years later, the same question was being asked in the United States of America:
"Why should Communists and/or Fascists demand toleration when their real aim is to overthrow the government which tolerates them?" And in our time, too, intellectuals could not necessarily be trusted to be more
tolerant than other men; it is certain that many of them
have taken strong sides in these issues. During the
period of the rise and fall of Puritanism, John Milton
also took sides, and demanded freedom of the press for
everyone except Papists. (It is to be remembered that
from the time Henry VIII established a national church
of England until perhaps late in the eighteenth century,
Popery and Papists represented to Englishmen the threat
of a militant foreign power. During the era of Queen
Elizabeth, this militant foreign power was Spain; later
it was France. To Englishmen in the period of Cromwell
and Milton, both Spain and France were as dangerous to
the national existence as Russia seems dangerous to ours

today. "The Papist" was the man with the sword and the cloak; the Papist occupied exactly the same place in the public mind as our picture of the bomb-throwing Communist does today. And, as it is today, some of the fear, based on the potential aggressiveness of a foreign power, was realistic; a great deal of it was hysterical.)

John Milton objected to censorship of the press because, among other reasons, he had discovered most censors to be a narrow and unimaginative lot.

> Lastly, I wrote my *Areopagitica* in order to deliver the press from the restraints with which it was encumbered; that the power of determining what was true and what was false, what ought to be published and what to be suppressed, might no longer be entrusted to a few illiterate and illiberal individuals, who refused their sanction to any work which contained views or sentiments at all above the level of the vulgar superstition.[13]

Milton recognized the backwoodsman, the civilization wrecker to be a man in a brocaded coat marked "official censorship." Yet Milton had his own limits; Roman Catholicism threatened him—he could not tolerate it. John Locke, in his *Letters on Toleration* could tolerate Papists and Protestants alike; but atheism threatened his moral security—he could not tolerate atheists. The First Marquess of Halifax (George Savile) called himself The Trimmer, and represented a different kind of civilized, verbal man than either John Locke or John Milton. He perfectly represented that period following any intense revolutionary, political, or religious ferment when men, growing sick to death of the fight, desire in Taylor's words, peace rather than truth. George Savile was a Restoration man, as sophisticated as Lorenzo de Medici but perhaps much less understanding. He adhered to the maxim, Do Not Believe Too Much in Anything, Therefore Tolerate Everything. Like all men of this stripe, Savile found it difficult to believe that men might believe in something a great deal, and yet still allow other men, who believe in opposing values, the right to "preach back again." Believing in nothing very much was the Marquess' way out of caring too much about what other men preached at all. But Savile was not unaware of the way things were. In his *Letter to a Dissenter*, he draws an exact line between loyalty to the church and loyalty to the state: "We all agree in our Duty to our Prince; our Objections to his Belief do not hinder us from seeing his Vertues; and our not complying with his Religion (Roman Catholicism) hath no effect upon our Allegiance."[14]

Charles II, the prince in question, was not so sure that distinctions of this kind were not drawing too thin a line. Gilbert Burnet reports that when at ease, Charles II "could not help letting himself out against the liberty that under the Reformation all men took of inquiring into matters of religion; for from their inquiring into matters of religion they carried the humor farther to inquire into matters of state."[15]

John Stuart Mill was even wiser than Charles II:

Yet so natural to mankind is intolerance in whatever they *really care about* that religious freedom has hardly anywhere been practically realized, except where religious indifference, which dislikes to have its peace disturbed by theological quarrels, has added its weight to the scale. . . . Wherever the sentiment of the majority is still genuine and intense, it is found to have abated little of its claims to be obeyed. The disposition of mankind, whether as rulers or as fellow-citizens, to impose their own opinions and inclinations as a rule of conduct on others, is as energetically supported by some of the best and by some of the worst feeling incident to human nature, that it is hardly ever kept under restraint by anything but want of power; and as the power is not declining, but growing, unless *a strong barrier of moral conviction* can be raised against the mischief, we must expect, in the present circumstances of the world, to see it increase.[16]

Trumbull Park—a History

South Deering, a neighborhood area in southeast Chicago, is a long peninsula of small homes, running from 100th to 126th Streets, and surrounded on one side by industry such as Wisconsin Steel and General Mills, and on the other by Lake Calumet, prairies, and railroad tracks. South Deering residents are of Polish, Lithuanian, and Slavic ethnic origin, many of them first- or second-generation immigrants. There are also a few Mexican-Americans living there, but until July 1953—absolutely no Negroes.

It was in this area in 1938 that the Public Works Administration built a housing project for low-income families called Trumbull Park Homes. Trumbull is now one of the twenty-six housing projects owned by the Chicago Housing Authority, which started operations in 1937 under the leadership of Miss Elizabeth Wood. For some years CHA has had, by law, a nondiscriminatory tenant-selection policy; in practice the law has not been enforced in several Authority projects because of the hostility of the surrounding neighborhoods to the tenancy of Negroes.

The policy might have gone unenforced for an indefinite period of time, except for one of those accidents which, on the surface, appears so unlikely as to strike all prejudiced observers as a deliberate "planting" of Negroes in the Trumbull Project.

The accident appeared one day during the summer of 1953 in the form of Betty Howard, an attractive and poised woman of 24, who went up to the Housing Authority office to be interviewed and to file an application for housing in Trumbull. Her husband, Donald Howard, was at work in the post office and could not accompany her for the interview. Everything was in order; Donald was a veteran, and in every other way the Howard family was eminently eligible for public housing.

On July 30, 1953, the Donald Howards and their two children, Cynthia, 4, and Donald, Jr., 3, moved into an apartment at 10630 South Bensley Avenue, Trumbull Park Homes. Nothing happened for several days, nor did

the Howards expect anything to happen, since they took
it for granted that all Chicago Housing Authority projects were interracial, just as the brochures said. And
nobody in the CHA expected anything to happen either,
because Betty Howard, who is sociologically Negro,
looks as white as the whitest second-generation Polish
woman walking through the streets of South Deering.
Betty's husband, Donald, was at first mistaken for a
Mexican-American—until it turned out that he didn't
speak Spanish.

A few days after the move-in, Donald Howard was
spotted by the residents of South Deering while on an
innocuous shopping trip in the area. On August 5 a crowd
of fifty South Deering residents and stray hangers-on
broke a window of the Howards' apartment. On August
9 there was more violence, and South Deering in that
long and extended Indian Summer of 1953 began to
resemble an occupied country; three shifts of 250 policemen were thrown around the project twenty-four hours a
day; aerial bombs exploded hour after hour; Donald and
Betty Howard were escorted to work in police vans, and
otherwise virtually confined to their apartment behind
sandbags and a cordon of police.

Arson occurred regularly. On August 27, a liquor
store in the vicinity was burned out, netting a $10,000
loss to the owner, who for ten years in the South Deering
community had served Negro and white citizens alike.
Across the street, at a catercornered angle from the liquor

store, stands a Catholic church, a highly influential institution in an area which is predominantly Catholic.
The priest of that church allegedly had been approached,
at the time the violence began, about "preaching a sermon on Brotherly Love." He had reportedly answered
that he could do no such thing without dangerously
jeapardizing the $80,000 worth of stained-glass windows
and other valuable church property under his care. Later,
Betty Howard, a Catholic, made several trips to church
in the company of white Catholic friends, and was repeatedly stoned on her way home by alleged co-religion-
ists from South Deering.

The Chicago Housing Authority, meanwhile, had no
choice but to adhere to state and federal laws prohibiting
discrimination in housing projects. The National Association for the Advancement of Colored People threatened the Authority with a suit for racial discrimination
in housing. Slowly, therefore, other Negro families followed the Howards into Trumbull.

It is agreed by many that, had the police nipped the disor-
ders in the very beginning, they would have been stopped
and not become chronic. The police did make some arrests
and, up to April first, 115 adults and 55 juveniles were ar-
rested. Convictions of adults have not been high . . . but this
is not necessarily the fault of the police. There have been
reports of a good deal of fraternization between the police
and the protesting residents of the community. . . . On April
21st (1954), a committee from the Council Against Discrimination met with top police officials and submitted a

specific list of evidence of inadequate policing. On May 7th, Police Commissioner Timothy O'Connor announced that the policing arrangements at the project and in the area would be modified.[17]

Meanwhile, the state of affairs in South Deering began to border on civil disobedience. Trumbull Park became the subject of articles in LIFE Magazine (November 9, 1953), TIME, EBONY, PAGEANT, COLLIER'S, and in national newspapers. Abroad, the continuing state of violence became a kind of *cause célèbre*: Trumbull was pointed out as an indication of the way in which Americans treat their nonwhite population.

In Chicago, the situation brought to focus the uneasy racial situation, the bad housing conditions, and the corrupt politics of the city, conditions not unlike those to be found in any large industrial center in the United States.

The housing situation itself has long been reason enough for explosion. At the time that the Howards moved into Trumbull, 13 per cent of the white population and 28 per cent of the Negroes in Chicago were living in "congested quarters." The Negro resident, with two-thirds the average income of the white, was paying almost as much rent as the average white resident. (Since it is far more difficult for Negroes to find places to live, they are forced to pay rents far out of line with the existing rental rates.) Because of discriminatory housing, the nonwhites who comprise 14 per cent of Chicago's total population have been pushed, crowded, bullied, and forced into a bare 11 per cent of the available housing in the city.[18]

The racial situation cannot be understood unless we are to examine the hate-distorted faces of the mobs—often composed chiefly of middle-aged women—caught by camera and television throwing rocks at moving vans as they brought in new Negro families to the project. It is easy enough to condemn their conduct as deplorable; it is not so easy to get behind their thinking, or lack of thought, and to sort out the reasons for it.

An ironic incident occurring in the first months of "The Trouble" might serve as an illustration. Following an arson in the South Deering area, several policemen were guarding the scene of the action; among them was a calm Negro policeman, who was subjected to jeers and insults by a group of shrill women watchers. The Negro at first kept a dignified silence.

"We wouldn't have no Gestapo on our neck now if it weren't for you old black things!" yelled one of the women.

Finally the Negro policeman answered: "Then go back to Europe if you don't like it here!"

The return jibe hit home; a good many South Deering residents are sensitive about not being as "American" as other people. South Deering is an area of home owners, of first- and second-generation Poles and Italians and Slovaks and Serbs who have piled dollar on dollar—

painfully—through the years, in order to buy their own homes. The heads of many of these families look forward to dying in their own homes, because that is very important to them; and they desire to leave their homes to their children. Because of their comparatively recent immigration, these people are conscious of having been very near to low-man on the social totem pole; many of the second generation are self-conscious about the fact that the Old Man or the Old Lady does not speak English very well. Long before the violence began, there had been a high degree of juvenile delinquency in the area; after it began the teen-age gangs had a socially approved reason for setting off their aerial bombs.

> Contrary to frequent assertions that immigrants contribute unduly to crime in the United States . . . statistical evidence indicates that immigrants tend to have a decidedly lower crime rate than old Americans (third or more generation in this country). The highest crime rate is found among second generation Americans, and is caused by the clash between old world standards represented by the parents and the new standards to which these second generation Americans are exposed. By and large, the first generation immigrants tend to live in the closely-knit, well-organized, immigrant communities of our large cities and have little social contact with other groups. Their children, however, go to American schools and are encouraged by them to seek the company of other children living outside the immigrant ghettoes. . . . The ultimate outcome of the conflict between the desire to do what (their) playmates do, the fear of ridicule in school, and parental punishment at home may lead to

revolt against the parents and perhaps even lead the child
to the bars of our juvenile courts.[19]

The people of South Deering are frightened and frustrated; and in their fear and frustration they are enraged.
They are enraged at the very idea of what they call
"Niggers." "Niggers" will rape their daughters, depreci-
ate the values of their hard-won homes, bring them slums.
These fears and hates are, of course, almost totally beyond the realm of reason. South Deering has created its
own reality. At one time neighborhood newspapers in
the area were suggesting in heavy-handed seriousness
that South Deering should secede from the city of Chicago.

Trumbull Park—the Moral Dilemma

The South African novelist, Alan Paton, made a trip to
Trumbull Park, and described it as an *unreal* world:

> It is fascinating to consider why the struggle between ideal
> and practice should be considered to be so especially Amer-
> ican. It is the American drama. One of the great scenes of
> it is being played today, in the theater of Trumbull Park. . . .
> You wouldn't have known it was Trumbull Park, if it
> hadn't been for the bombs going off in South Deering, and
> for the police everywhere at every turn, and for the fact that
> it was the white tenants sitting in the sun. The white tenants
> of the project take no active part in South Deering's fight
> against the Negroes; you learn that some do little kindnesses,
> and some are hostile, and most are cold. It's an unreal world,
> white children playing, white women staring, white and col-
> ored policemen smoking, colored men and women and chil-

dren sitting behind blinds, the sun shining and the trees coming out in leaf, and the bombs. The bombs don't go off all the time; sometimes they stop, and it's just when you think: "Maybe, maybe there'll be no more," that they go off again.

I met Mr. Herman King, one of the colored tenants, a veteran. He is a big man, and he talked to me quietly, but he talked to me like a man who has some deep internal pain, and wishes wistfully that it were not there, but that is how it is. Sometimes he stopped talking and looked out into space, which was not very far, because the blinds were down. . . .

I hardly spoke. I only listened. What can one say to such a man?

"Are you tired of talking?" I asked.

"Not to you," he said.

And what could I say? Why does he equate himself with me, who have never faced such things in my easy life. . . . [20]

Paton met Louis P. Dinnocenzo, president of the South Deering Improvement Association, who at the beginning of the summer of 1954 was quoted in the *Chicago Daily News* as saying, "The people haven't begun to fight. As soon as the weather breaks, there will be a lot more violence.[21]

(Dinnocenzo) says, "Let them take the Negroes out of here. Then let us re-educate the people. Then maybe the Negroes can come back."

He is supported by *The Daily Calumet* (circulation: 11,-000) and its redoubtable editor, Colonel Horace F. Wulf. The colonel is American and Christian too, and is for brotherhood. His argument about brotherhood is very clear:

1. Brotherhood is a fine thing.
2. It fights against odds of greed and human nature.
3. You cannot enforce it by law.
4. It begins with the "rank and file, not in the mighty houses of state."
5. Therefore support the Scouts, YMCA, clubs, and churches.
6. But do not try to enforce it by law. . . . [22]

It was the South Deering Improvement Association, with the backing of *The Daily Calumet* (until recently owned and operated by Colonel Wulf), which provided the organizational impetus for the constant, daily, and planned disturbance in Trumbull Park. On the organizational end, these groups were aided by (1) the White Circle League, led in Chicago by a fanatic man named Joseph Beauharnais. A notorious group, the White Circle League puts out circulars with the slogan, "A Dead Nigger Is a Good Nigger." (2) The National Citizens Protective Association, organized by John W. Hamilton, a long-time associate of the American fascist, Gerald L. K. Smith.

But these creators of conspiracy within the body politic have been often reinforced by larger forces within the city of Chicago and within the United States: real estate groups which make money by forcing Negroes to pay higher rents for poorer dwellings; the political administration of the city of Chicago; the social conflicts of immigrant groups. A little more than a year after the Trumbull riots began, Elizabeth H. Wood was fired as executive secretary of the Chicago Housing Authority. Miss Wood was by any standards an extraordinary woman. A former teacher of English at Vassar, Elizabeth Wood had entered the field of housing during the pioneer days of 1937. As executive director of the CHA, she was the kind of administrator who did not lose pioneering enthusiasm; she was also the kind of administrator who managed, for seventeen years, to keep the CHA free of political and financial scandal. (And the Chicago Housing Authority was one of the few institutions in the City of which this could be truthfully said.)

Technically, Elizabeth Wood was fired on the grounds that business considerations were more important than the "social aspects" of the CHA. The reason for her dismissal, was, of course, part of the Trumbull Park story.

There were other elements of course: the enmity of politi cians who failed to win favors from her; the thousands of pe tition signatures presented at the City Hall demanding her dismissal, collected by anti-public-housing groups as well as lunatic-fringe organizations. A tragic footnote is the fac that there was never a word uttered in support of Miss Wood by the man most obligated to utter it—the mayor. (Martin Kennelly.)

City Hall is thinking about other matters: the mayoral and aldermanic elections of next spring. In a sense, dumping Elizabeth Wood helps clear the decks for Kennelly to run again. He is in a better position for political fence mending especially with Chicago's South Side bloc of aldermen—and can better face the mass of property-owning voters with their deep-rooted fears of falling property values in a changing city. Did Kennelly alienate the liberal voter? That voter is in the minority and dislikes the present Democratic régime anyway. The Negro vote? It is imponderable.

Miss Wood was more than "Miss Public Housing" on the Chicago scene. She was among the last of that group of governmental servants of the mid-'30's—the Ickeses and the Hopkinses—whose integrity, devotion to public service, and belief in the principles upon which the nation was founded, could never be swayed by "realistic" politicians. This was her undoing.[23]

Today, civil disobedience in South Deering is in its third year. The people of South Deering (not all the people but a good many, and those white citizens who don't go along with the violence can be terrorized into silence) have built up a pattern of both open and secret resistance to law. For these people Elizabeth Wood has been a focal point of hatred: an independent do-gooder, a woman bent in foisting upon them a sinister "conspiracy." It is not part of the South Deering scheme of things that Elizabeth Wood could be chiefly interested in enforcing a law forbidding discrimination.

Meanwhile, too, the "good" people of Chicago remain ineffective, for the good people have been either too weak or too apathetic; long ago they let some of the most important aspects of their city life slide into the hands of gangsters or politicians connected with gangsters. Every child in the city of Chicago knows that you can run any kind of business you want to in the city if you pay off to the proper people at the right times.

And the deep schism between American ideology and American practice continues. In the same year that South Deering broke into rioting, the Supreme Court handed down the historic decision outlawing the segregation of Negro and white pupils in the public school system of the United States. Law is on the side of Herman King, but in South Deering it cannot keep—or has not kept—him and his wife and children from being threatened with murder. Law has so far been unable to help the best-qualified American Negro to get a good job; for all Negroes in the United States are subjected to the cold maxim, "last hired, first fired." Only the *enforcement* of the law—which is much different from mere enactment of the law—and heavily enforced social sanctions against discrimination can do that.

> In spite of widespread anti-Semitic propaganda in Germany the boycott of Jews after Hitler's rise to power was a partial failure *until legislation succeeded in segregating Jews and gentiles completely.* . . . Contrary to co-operation, toleration usually implies conflict. Such conflict may exist between the individual's prejudice and his democratic belief in equality and fairness; or it may represent the outcome of a conflict between his prejudices and his need to give in to the demands of an unprejudiced environment. In the latter case, a lessening of the curbs imposed by the environment, a decline in societal sanctions against prejudice, may change tolerance to overt discrimination. . . . [24]

At least forty-five million Americans are subject to discrimination at one time or another, with the chief targets being members of the colored races (about fifteen million), Jews (about five million), and Catholics (about twenty-five million).[25] But by far the worst discriminatory practices have so far been meted out to the colored minorities; in the South these practices are reinforced by segregation laws; in the North these practices are modified by occasional state-enforced fair employment legislation (most notably in New York state) and by laws forbidding discrimination against the seating or serving of Negroes in public places. In so far as these antidiscriminatory laws are to some extent enforced, and in so far as social sanctions against prejudice grow stronger, it might be said that in the North in general more conflict does exist between "the individual's prejudice and his democratic belief in equality and fairness." And in so far as this conflict does exist, Alan Paton is justified in stating that "the struggle between ideal and practice should be considered to be so especially American."

> The American democratic ideal says: All men are equal before the law. The Law is impartial.
>
> The American reality says: If you've got influence, or if your father's a big man, you can get off cheap.
>
> The Judeo-Christian ethic says: Love thy brother as thyself.
>
> The American reality says: "I'm a Catholic . . . and a good one, I'd say. But the church hasn't got a right to tell me

who I should live next to. And the church knows it, too,
because it hasn't said anything about Trumbull Park."[26]

The civilized tradition says: "The confidence which even the
poor man feels when he closes behind him the door of his
dark, cold, damp hovel, changes the whole outlook of a
man. . . . Until I came to England the appearance of a
police officer in a house where I was living always produced an indefinable disagreeable feeling, and I was at
once morally on my guard against an enemy. In England
a policeman at your door merely adds to your sense of
security."[27]

The American reality says: "The Howards sought a home.
They got bombs, curses, smashing glass."[28]

How can reality be changed? The reality can be changed
through the pressure of law—and of social sanction, for
most people in the United States are willing to obey the
law; and most people desire sanction from their fellows
for their acts. In a good many cases social sanction goes
hand in hand with law; that is, the law of the time reflects
the mores of the time. Trumbull Park represents, among
other things, a strong local social sanction in opposition
to law. At Trumbull Park, indeed, we see as important a
phenomenon as can be observed anywhere in the United
States or in the world: rule outside of law. The rioters in
South Deering are saying an important and dangerous
thing: We are outside of society; we adhere to our own
sanctions; we take the law into our own hands. The
rioters at Trumbull, furthermore, accomplished an ex-
ceedingly dangerous thing: they succeeded in making

the police, supposedly upholders of the law, their tacit accomplices in subversion of the law. John Brown and the abolitionists were also violators of the Southern law of slavery; but John Brown—like a good many martyrs —violated the law in the name of a higher morality, rather than in the name of the kind of narrow and sectional loyalty upheld by the South Deering rioters.

The important point to grasp here is the difference between laws made in the name of universal human morality (thou shalt not kill) and those created in the name of temporary vigilante passion or of immediate group self-interest (thou shalt not kill except when threatened economically or emotionally). It is not a question, as Colonel Wulf would try to tell us, of "legislating brotherhood"; rather, it is a question of legislating for—and enforcing—first-class citizenship for all the people of the United States.

Brotherhood may indeed be more difficult than citizenship. Brotherhood, that sense of *agape* with all human life, is perhaps given only to some rare temperaments; brotherhood in that deepest sense requires an understanding of sin and of goodness, a realization of humanness, which most of us cannot live up to. But the sense of justice is a quality which needs not be foreign to any of us.

Government by Law

If rule by law is one of the oldest and most important

of the great traditions of Western man, it is also a slow and painfully developed tradition. Most of us are familiar with that long process of thought and trial which finally flowered into the ideas of habeas corpus, of restrictive police powers, of trial by a jury of peers rather than trial by fire, rope climbing, or the arbitrary will of one man or one vigilante group.

The laws of men change; the ideals of law and of justice under law do not change.

> . . . The rules are part of the game. They are not outside of it. No rule, then no game; different rules, then a different game. . . . In the second place, an individual may at times feel that a decision isn't fair and he may even get angry. *But he is not objecting to a rule* but to what he claims is a violation of it, to some one-sided and unfair action. . . . In the third place, the rules . . . have the sanction of tradition and precedent . . . the authority . . . in question is not a manifestation of a merely personal will; the parent or teacher exercises it as the representative and agent of the interests of the group as a whole. . . . This makes the difference between action which is arbitrary and that which is just and fair.[29]

Strict adherence to the law by itself may, as Jesus of Nazareth so skillfully pointed out when he broke the Sabbath rules by working, become an empty and hollow thing. The most skillfully constructed constitution does not in itself protect democracy from becoming a tyranny.

Tyranny at its best is still rule without laws and, according to Socrates' definition, justice is identical with legality or obedience to laws. . . . The laws which determine what is legal are the rules of conduct upon which the citizens have agreed. "The citizens" may be "the multitude" or "the few." . . . That is to say, the laws, and hence what is legal, depend on the political order of the community for which they are given. . . . Absolute rule of a man who knows how to rule, who is a born ruler, is actually superior to the rule of laws, in so far as the good ruler is a "seeing law," and laws do not "see," or legal justice is blind. Whereas a good ruler is necessarily beneficient, laws are not necessarily beneficient. To say nothing of laws which are actually bad and harmful, even good laws suffer from the fact that they cannot "see." . . . Tyrannical rule as well as "constitutional" rule will be legitimate to the extent to which the tyrant or the "constitutional" rulers will listen to counsel of him who "speaks well" because he "thinks well."[30]

This classic conception of good government as a government advised, counseled, or run by wise men is not a part of the modern American's ideological framework. He would consider tyranny—even if tyranny were the rule of a great and wise man—to be categorically bad. But the very impersonality of law—as an ideal—constitutes its "blindness," its impartiality. Law is more than written statutes. It is tradition. It is property rights and human rights. It is fault finding and blame laying; ideally, too, it is the protection of the citizen. It gives no favoritism to any man, ideally, even though he has property and is a man of parts. The law does not ask *why* a

man commits murder; it only asks, *did* he? The motive
is important only so long as it establishes more definite
evidence for the act.

As we have pointed out, the men who settled the
frontier were not much more interested than Huckleberry
Finn in this impersonal idea of justice. But while Huckleberry Finn would adhere to a higher morality of the
universal heart (at the risk always of being *outside* of
society) most frontiersmen took comfort from a parochial and immediate sense of vengeance—a law more
closely akin to an eye for an eye than to any large idea
of constitutionalism. In the South, as W. J. Cash points
out, this immediate and passionately personal approach
to law survived long after the geographical frontier was
over:

> Nor was it only private violence that was thus perpetuated.
> The Southerner's fundamental approach carried over into
> the realm of public offenses as well. What the direct willful-
> ness of his individualism demanded, when confronted by a
> crime that aroused his anger, was immediate satisfaction for
> itself—catharsis for personal passion in the spectacle of a
> body dancing at the end of a rope or writhing in the fire—
> now, within the hour—and *not some ponderous abstract jus-
> tice in a problematic tomorrow.* And so, in this world of in-
> effective social control, the tradition of vigilante action, which
> normally lives and dies with the frontier, not only sur-
> vived but grew so steadily that already long before the Civil
> War and long before hatred for the black man had begun to
> play any direct part in the pattern (of more than three

hundred persons said to have been hanged or burned by mobs between 1840 and 1860, less than ten per cent were Negroes) the South had become peculiarly the home of lynching.[31]

Thus, the conflict between two ideas of law—as well as the conflict between two opposing cultures and two economic systems—came to a head in the Civil War. For the settlers of the original Thirteen Colonies had been as legalistic as the Southerners were passionate, parochial, and arbitrary. The Puritans, "the most intellectual and articulate of the seventeenth-century settlers" in the New World, arrived in America with a highly developed concept of aristocratic right and duty. The Puritans "had no exalted opinion of human nature. For the most part they believed in the moral right and practical necessity of authority and rank, in both church and state. Men, according to the Puritan creed, were not by nature either reasonable or good and they were certainly not born equals. . . . Most of them clung to the belief that ordinary mortals needed instruction, guidance, perhaps even coercion, by their enlightened and duly designated leaders."[32]

Dissidents from any given colony ruled in any given way had an entire continent in which to knock about freely. When Roger Williams was banished from Massachusetts Bay, he simply moved fifty miles away, bought land from the Indians, and set up a colony based on the separation of the church and state. In this manner, the early colonies came to have a wide divergence of concepts: theocracy, oligarchy, enlightened tyranny, liberal democracy. Legislators in any particular colony might act according to biblical law, common law, natural law, or (and especially when the frontier won out) simple expediency.

Out of this welter of European governmental and legal traditions came the Thirteen Colonies, united in revolt *against* something. It is generally supposed by latter-day Americans that the colonies made common cause against a bad king, who in both his kingship and his inadequacy, represented the monarchist principle. This is not strictly true. The colonies were fighting chiefly the idea of being colonies at all; that is, they were fighting the principle of colonialism, a colonialism promulgated by "an omnicompetent Parliament at Westminster . . . (which) now controlled the Executive, and, moreover, claimed to control the colonies too."[33] Now colonialism always means, in essence, just about the same thing: that the colonial territories shall be tied economically and politically (but especially economically) to the needs and demands of the mother country.

Since the right of revolution against any kind of authority—including colonialism—is nowhere clear, and since the new aristocracies which controlled the governments of the separate colonies were composed of traditionalists, it appeared as a duty and a compulsion to these traditionalists to make their right to take up arms, not only clear, but justifiable. Thus the apology: "a decent respect to the opinions of mankind." Men such as George Washington and John Adams were part of the process of aristocratic government, well acquainted with the intricacies of legal and economic management; they could not afford to set up a structure for revolution which might be turned, in time, against them or their kind of government. It was the revolutionary liberals—people such as Sam Adams, Tom Paine, Thomas Jefferson—who "intended that principles put forward to justify resistance to an oppressive régime in England should be applied also to justify attacks on the authority of colonial aristocracies."[34]

The men who signed the Declaration of Independence were objecting to the things from which most colonial groups suffer: "for cutting off our trade with all parts of the world; for imposing taxes on us without our consent; for depriving us in many cases of the benefits of trial by jury; raising the conditions of new appropriations of lands; for quartering large bodies of armed troops among us. . . ." Most of these signers would have been unhappy to have been identified with the French revolutionists, those terrorists, those "men without britches." It was only after home rule for the colonies had been established—that is, only after the Declaration of Independence had been put into effect through force of arms —that the framers of the Constitution divided openly into left and right on the question of how the nation

should be governed. The Constitution itself was not a
new idea in the world.

> Justice, tranquillity, defense, welfare, these are ends an-
> nounced by all governments. No government ever existed, ex-
> cept perhaps that of Nazi Germany, which would have ad-
> mitted that it meant to disregard any one of these ends. But
> the last purpose, that of securing liberty, was wholly new.
> There had been formal written constitutions before, but no
> government ever before had been created of which the final
> and overruling purpose was that of securing liberty.[35]

Liberty under law, then, was the concept which distinguished the American constitution as a unique thing.
It was embodied in a highly formalistic and legalistic
document for many of the reasons we have already men-
tioned, among them the fact that the young independent
colonies, having almost no traditions not borrowed from
Europe, could not depend, as the English have done, on
an unwritten body of common law. Two things concerning the Constitution we should touch on here, even though
briefly: the concept of liberty under law and the concept
of checks and balances.

> Calvin's distrust of pure democracy, his wise words in favor
> of a mixed form of government, which combined monarchic
> and aristocratic leadership with democratic participation,
> was . . . incorporated . . . in the Constitution of the United
> States of America. Even the salutary doctrine of checks and
> balances . . . owes something to the Calvinist distrust of the
> claims of centralized authority and its pessimistic insight
> into the inevitable corruptions of human pride.[36]

Rule by Man

Vigilante rule is the sheer expression of human pride and unbridled human passion; constitutional rule, as it was envisaged in one form or another by the framers of the American constitution, was a curbing of human passion and pride through the enforcement of an abstract code with the backing, of course, of the inevitable resort to force. The enforcement of the right to liberty, however, is, as we have seen, one of the most difficult and ticklish of all legal or governmental problems. In its insistence on the principle of liberty under law (and the corollary doctrine of checks and balances) the American constitution was one of the highest flowerings of eighteenth and nineteenth century liberal democracy.

> Liberalism is that principle of political rights, according to which the public authority, in spite of being all-powerful, limits itself and attempts, even at its own expense, to leave room in the State over which it rules for those to live who neither think nor feel as it does, that is to say as do the stronger, the majority. Liberalism—it is well to recall this today—is the supreme form of generosity. . . . It announces the determination to share existence with the enemy; more than that, with an enemy which is weak. It was incredible that the human species should have arrived at so noble an attitude, so paradoxical, so refined, so acrobatic, so antinatural. Hence, it is not to be wondered at that this same humanity should soon appear anxious to get rid of it. It is a discipline too difficult and complex to take firm root on earth.[37]

Thus, some of the strongest defenders of civil liberties in our hard-pressed times are those staunch conservatives or unflinching old-line liberals who still adhere to the principle that liberty should be enforced by law. This means *not their liberties only, but the liberties of other men.* This principle can be understood on two levels, the ethical (what is done to my brother is also done to me) and the pragmatic (that which reduces some members of the community to second-class citizenship will eventually threaten to reduce me also).

All men in our country who adhere to these basic principles of democracy are threatened both ethically and pragmatically by the continuance of the situation in South Deering. To take a more famous example, such men were mortally threatened by the outcome of the Sacco-Vanzetti case.

In brief, the outlines of this case were as follows: On August 27, 1927, after seven years of trials and retrials, two semiliterate Italian immigrants—Nicola Sacco and Bartolomeo Vanzetti—were executed in Boston for a murder which almost everyone now admits they could not have committed. Sacco and Vanzetti were avowed and passionate anarchists. They represented not merely an unpopular radical ideology but also a not necessarily popular ethnic minority.

The case of Sacco and Vanzetti was at once the glory and the tragedy, the triumph and the disaster of American social protest in this century. No other cause would seem so pure; no other protagonists would glow so much like walking flames. To have been in the Sacco-Vanzetti death watch was, for one time in a man's life, to have walked almost alone among the heights. . . .

. . . In the summer of 1927 Bernard DeVoto, then a Harvard instructor, walked about Boston and set down what he saw and heard in *We Accept with Pleasure*, a novel published seven years later. One of his characters is a defense lawyer who asks in the last hours:

> "Who is it that is killing the poor wops? I wish I knew. Is it City or just the Hill? . . . Taxi drivers, newsboys, washerwomen, subway guards. . . . I ask them all. It's always "Hang the bastards."[38]

So deeply did national cleavage over the case run that the novelist, John Dos Passos—who along with such old-line liberals as DeVoto, Gardner Jackson, Edna St. Vincent Millay, Powers Hapgood, H. L. Mencken, Frank Sibley, helped run the Sacco-Vanzetti defense committee —later cried in despair:

> America our nation has been beaten by strangers who have turned our language inside out and who have taken the clean words our fathers spoke and made them slimy and foul.
>
> All right, we are two nations.[39]

In his novel, *Boston*, Upton Sinclair saw the Sacco-Vanzetti case as a crushing defeat for these old-line American liberals, and a victory for the Communists. Kempton, in illustration of this point, quotes one of the revolutionary characters in *Boston* who cries:

"Don't you see the glory of this case, it kills off the liberals! Before this, it was possible to argue that injustice was an accident, just an oversight—in a country that was busy making automobiles and bathtubs and books of etiquette. But now here's a test—we settle the question forever! We take our very best—not merely cheap politicians but great ones! Our supreme court justices—even the liberal ones! We prove them all alike—they know what flag they serve under, who serves out their rations!"[40]

And indeed, more and more, following the execution of Sacco and Vanzetti, did many thinking Americans ask, "Who is behind this particular law? What group does it benefit and what groups does it not benefit?" That the ideal of justice and of liberty under law could actually be enforced on the American scene became a matter of skepticism or of heartbreak for those who most believed in the formal constitutional code. These liberals knew, as Upton Sinclair points out, that injustice is indeed sometimes an accident. They knew that the formal legal code, although "blind" in the sense that all written principles are blind and impartial, could never possibly be put into effect by jurors and judges, (who no matter how deeply impartial they might attempt to be were still afflicted with the fact of being human). The humanity of jurors or judges, indeed, might work on the side of clemency, mercy, understanding, rather than on the side of harshness. For example, in a study of jury voting behavior being conducted under the auspices of the Uni-

versity of Chicago Law School, thirty experimental
juries, picked at random from the jury pools of the Chicago and St. Louis circuit and superior courts, showed
the following tendencies:

> Jurors with a minority group membership generally tended
> to vote for the plaintiff in personal injury cases and award
> higher verdicts. It is suggested that one of the reasons for
> this relationship is the direct result of the values generally
> held by a minority group. Briefly, these values are a) a
> tendency to empathize with the party who is seeking redress
> of grievance for maltreatment, especially if the complainant
> is a single individual and the negligent party a corporative
> body; b) the belief that the laws of society are superimposed
> by members of the majority and that these laws may be used
> to legitimate injustice; c) a generalized hostility towards
> what are defined as external symbols of authority, be it a
> courtroom or a cop on the beat.
>
>   . . . I am not suggesting that a person who belongs to a
> minority ethnic group consciously seeks to subvert the for-
> mal legal code when he is given the opportunity to serve as
> a juror. I am suggesting that because of his relatively low
> status and out-group position he will tend to have greater
> understanding with parties seeking redress of grievances
> and will tend to use the legitimate means at his disposal to
> rectify an injustice. From our data we see this most clearly
> among the Negroes, a minority group whose status is at the
> very low end of the continuum and whose verdicts are the
> highest.[41]

It was not, then, the fact that the administration of the
law is by the very nature of things *human*, that hurt so

deeply those men who had been in the Sacco-Vanzetti death watch. It was not even the fact that, as everyone knows, laws are often made by and for special interest groups.[42] Rather, it was that terrible combination of inflamed mob rancor ("hang the bastards") and either fear or corruption in the halls of justice ("not merely cheap politicians but great ones!") which so deeply impressed liberals. This was not a mistake, not a miscarriage of justice—but a direct subversion of justice, aided by hysteria, hatred, fear, and the desire for blood. Is it any wonder that Maxwell Anderson in his play, "Winterset," presents the Sacco-Vanzetti story as a tragedy, the legal outlines of which are obscured by the human horror?

Ironically enough, Sacco and Vanzetti themselves escaped less scathed in one sense than many of the liberals who took up their cause. As anarchists, neither of the accused and defamed men expected justice at the hands of their ideological enemies. Having had no hopes, they suffered little disillusion. And Vanzetti, in his last speech to the court, was able to transmute his own tragedy into the larger human tragedy, able to forget the laws of men in the concept of a larger moral universe:

> I have talk a great deal of myself, but I even forget to name Sacco.
>
> Sacco is a worker, a good worker, with a good job and good pay, a good and lovely wife, two beautiful children, and a neat little home in a wood, near a brook.

Sacco is a heart, a faith, a character, a man,
A man, lover of all mankind, who gave all, who sacrifice
    all . . .

O yes, it may be true, as some have put it, that I am more
    witful than he, a better babbler.
But how many times when hearing his heartfelt voice ring
    out a faith sublime,
I have had to stop my heart from trobbling to my throat
So as not to weep before him: this man called thief, and
    assassin, and doomed.

But Sacco's name will live in the hearts of the people when
    Katzmann's bones and yours are interred by time;
And when your names are but dim remembrances of a cursed
    past when man was wolf to the man. . . .

If it had not been for this thing, we would have live out
    our lives talking on streetcorners to scorning men; we
    would have die unknown, unmarked, failures.
Now we are not failures.
Never in our whole life could we hope to do such work for
    justice, for tolerance, for man's understanding of man
    as now we do by accident.
Our lives, our pains, our words—nothing.
The taking of our lives—lives of a good fisherman and a
    poor peddlar—everything.

That last agony is our triumph.

---

Chapter 4

*This is a world of compensation, and he who would
be no slave must consent to have no slave. Those
who deny freedom for others deserve it not for
themselves.*—ABRAHAM LINCOLN

Government by Men
and Government by Lobby

M EN profess democracy and democratic values, but
they fear them. Here again such a paradox presents a
baffling situation in self-government, as described in this
chapter in the two stories about the Chicago Teachers'
Union and the Automobile Workers of America. Public
opinion as a massive group wields powerful influence
over the individual's attitudes. It cuts across special interest or pressure groups and in spite of, or perhaps
because of, its fickleness, can suddenly rise to the defense of certain basic beliefs. The practice of lobbying
—the minority influence on the majority—is in itself
paradoxical, for its power can be used for good or for
evil, or for both at the same time. How can men in government be trained to use their powers wisely, to make
no compromise with conscience?

The Teachers' Union[1]
Local No. 1 of the Chicago Teachers' Union was the

product of external pressures—the payless paydays of
the Depression, and the political prostitution of the
schools beginning with Big Bill Thompson and extend-
ing through the Kelly-Nash machine era. During this
period, the teachers of Chicago had no organization to
represent them; at least half a dozen groups vied toward teacher leadership, and the fighting which ensued
took quite as much energy as did opposing the common
employer.

Out of desperation the teachers finally united, and for
the next six years they were more unity- than union-
minded. Their leader during the payless paydays, and
to some extent the founder of the union, was a man
named John Fewkes. Young, handsome, physically fear-
less, Fewkes had the support of the elementary school
teachers, the Men's Teachers' Union, the playground
teachers, and others who, as might be supposed, desired
leadership devoted to action and not analysis. Fewkes
was opposed by the Federation of Women High School
Teachers and others who looked upon teaching as a creative career rather than just another job. Like many other
constitutions, that of the Teachers' Union was a compromise between the action-oriented and the creation-
minded. The constitution provided for the election of a
president who stayed in the classroom and an executive
secretary who carried out policy. Thus, in reality, the
union started out with two executives and continued in
that condition for six years, or until I was fired as executive secretary.

My first extracurricular activity as a union function-
ary was to begin a study group on the relations between
the union, the city, the state, and the world. Though I
believed that proper interest in democracy could exist
only in proportion to one's ability to do something about
it, I was not of the opinion that what happened outside
Chicago was beyond our sphere of interest. I ran an-
nouncement of the organization and first meeting of the
study class in our journal, *The Chicago Union Teacher.*
The story ran a description of the aims of the class and
included a bibliography which listed Karl Marx's *Das
Kapital* among the suggested readings. I was soon waited
upon and reminded that to list such a reading was offen-
sive to certain members of the union who were unable
to discern between reading and believing.

Our study class was composed of the intellectually
curious and imaginative; within six months it was labeled as the "left" of the union. An innocent enough left,
I might add; but there is always something subversive-
seeming about ideas. In a hierarchical monolith, as I
later learned, a man can do all the educating he desires
as long as he sticks to the practical problems of wages
and hours, but very little if he attempts to analyze either
the nature of society or the nature of the institution with
which he is associated.

As executive secretary of the union I was almost con-
tinually brought into contact with authorities in both the
Board of Education and the American Federation of

Labor. Through these contacts I picked up information pertinent to teacher welfare, and I began to learn that information in the broad sense is not only that which is the by-product of abstract decision; it can also be a source of power. At that time the Teachers' Union had two legislative bodies: the executive board and an advisory board. Each body met at regular intervals and the president and the executive secretary reported to them on their stewardship. Each of them used the information secured from our contacts as a basis for these reports. Now sovereign bodies have a right to such information only by virtue of their special decision-making power. Since, in the Chicago Teachers' Union, the president and the executive secretary were the agents of decision, it was their duty to bring to bear all information which oriented around that decision. However, for Mr. Fewkes and his advisers there was always something mysterious about information and its dissemination; you got the feeling that though they told a lot, they always held back the more juicy bits.

Meanwhile, I was talking more freely to my study class than I was supposed to, simply because I believed information to be a matter of education and not manipulation. As a result, my study group members were often better informed than their elected counterparts in the legislative bodies. I had come to the conclusion that if people must make their decisions through their representatives, there is no way in the world for them to act wisely if information is limited or withheld. And the collective judgment of many is more to be trusted than that of any single person puffed up by the importance of making decisions in secrecy or outright conspiracy.

During my incumbency in the CTU, we had a membership of some eight thousand teachers in over three hundred schools. In the larger high schools there were active members who carried out their responsibilities, and through reports and bulletins the membership was fairly well informed. In the smaller schools, inadequately represented in the CTU, this was not the case. There was a need to carry the story of the union to its membership. To this end, I went from school to school, ate lunch with the teachers, answered their questions as directly as I knew how. In the first two years—before the program was curtailed—I talked with several hundred teachers. I discovered that many of the teachers were not too interested, and preferred to go about their daily tasks of checking in and checking out unmolested by greater concerns. For them the union was little more than an office at 509 South Wabash, in the same way that the Board of Education was something at 228 N. LaSalle and far removed from any of their daily concerns. As one teacher asked me: "Aren't you being paid to look after our interests and not to run around?" On another occasion, I was congratulating the teachers of a particular school for a decisive union parade by comparing this action with the sit-down strikes of the auto workers.

The response was instantaneous. I was assured vehemently that these Chicago teachers had nothing in common with the Reds in the CIO!

At this time I was encouraging meetings of various professional groups, meetings which sometimes so stimulated the teachers that they began to involve themselves in the interunion power struggle. This struggle focused around John Fewkes and myself, as leaders of the two opposed factions. The core of the Fewkes support lay in the elementary schools among teachers, shop, and playground instructors who had come up through the public or parochial schools (often through the receipt of political favors). My support came from the high school, college, and other teachers with a liberal arts background.

In the second year of my service with CTU, we had set up an educational conference for the purpose of introducing teachers to the most daring ideas in the field of education, and of inviting to the conference those community leaders who shared this interest.

We organized a speakers' bureau and built a contact list all over the city to enable the PTA and other women's groups to take the story of the union to the teachers in their communities. I went to all kinds of meetings in order to interpret the day-by-day problems with which we were faced. Objections to these activities were expressed in the following logic: Is not the Chicago Teachers' Union identified with the Chicago Federation of Labor? Does not the Chicago Federation of Labor hold a powerful position with the city politicians? Shouldn't, therefore, all grievances be channeled through the Chicago Federation of Labor and ultimately to the president of the Board? Isn't this the way in which the carpenters, plumbers, bricklayers, and so on, achieved the protection of their membership? Or, still more bluntly: "Grow up. Don't waste your energies circuit-riding. Get acquainted with the power boys and protect our interests."

Thus the two heads of the teachers' union began to go their own ways: one to see Joe Keenan and John Fitzpatrick of the AFL; the other to the people. It was this divergent point of view which ultimately precipitated the showdown between Mr. Turley, successor to Fewkes, and myself. A conflict was inevitable between the two points of view: one insistent on a situation in which leadership bargained, and the hierarchy supported the bargains made; the other, desirous of a situation in which more and more people would be stimulated to act because their interest was projected into the welfare of the school, community, and city.

I had reached the conclusion that periodic turnover in policy-making positions within the union structure is advisable; and that those who represent the workers and teachers should have their ideals protected by never being paid more on a monthly basis than the category of workers they represent. (For example, since I was a high school teacher and since I served the teachers through a twelve-month year, I should have been paid the equivalent of a high school teacher's salary for a twelve-month year with a one-month vacation.) I also began to feel that all expenses should be carefully itemized, and since the employees of unions live off dues, these employees should exhibit certain sensitivities in regard to how the workers' money is spent. Further, I believed that all union elections needed to be contested, and that they could only be contested by real rivalry for each position.

Now the political supporters of Mr. Fewkes believed —and rightfully so—that the burden of being both a president of the union and a teacher in the classroom was too great. From the beginning, the Fewkes faction drove for an amendment of the constitution which would no longer make it mandatory that the president remain a classroom teacher. Later, the constitution was further amended to make possible—for all practical purposes— the permanent succession of an office holder. With no rivalry for the office of president, the teachers' union has become much like all other unions or groups which have uncontested elections.

Meanwhile, during the time that a contest still prevailed, conflict between the Fewkes and Eby faction was inevitable. The conflict was finally brought into the open at a teachers' convention in Gary, Indiana, in 1942. The showdown, like all other showdowns, was personalized; in this case through the firing of Eby and the vindication of Fewkes. Or rather, the vindication of Fewkes and his ultimate firing through political overthrow.

My contract provided for a hearing with an appeal before the House of Representatives of the Teachers' Union. The vote in the executive board was eighteen for firing and eleven against, with a two-thirds majority needed. After all the evidence was in, no minds were changed and the vote remained the same. Each group felt the other a threat to its existence. In the appeal to the House of Representatives, a broader base was fought out on the same lines. There the powers were more evenly balanced and the point of view which I represented would have prevailed except for one of those intriguing quirks of history. The actual Left, that is, the Communists, controlled some five votes directly and eleven indirectly, and they voted with the right because of annoyance at the center's consistent attacks on the Kelly-Nash machine in Chicago; this machine supported Roosevelt, and Roosevelt had just come back from Yalta. (A phenomenon which has also had its influence on a larger historical stage.)

For some years after my dismissal, a two-party system still prevailed in the union; the progressive caucus wielded real influence and at one point in its history came within two hundred votes of capturing the union. Today their influence is gone, however, and they meet only as a social group. The machine is in control once and for all.

Why? The answers are manifold. I shall give only a few. We were too naïve. We did not know how to organize. We wanted to widen our base, but we loved ideas more than intrigue. The pattern we set in the union was contradictory to the hierarchical patterns of the unions with which we were affiliated and with the city political structure. Our pattern bucked the institutional pattern.

These are all important reasons, but what really killed our dreams were the teachers themselves who, while professing democracy and democratic values, feared them. They preferred authority. They preferred to be told. They were afraid of freedom because they were afraid of life. When they came into power they were hard taskmasters; when they won the power to hire and fire, they could not trust others because they could not trust themselves. They wanted tenure for themselves against their employers' whims, but when the teachers themselves became employers, they demanded the retention of the power to hire and fire. For wouldn't they protect those who protected the union? The office girls didn't need a union, for if they organized they would reflect on their bosses. Nor were the office girls treated as equals, for secretaries were never quite so important in the scheme of things as teachers. The teachers, themselves victims of an authoritarian relationship, could find release only as they projected a similar pattern downward.

Later, in the Congress of Industrial Organizations, I learned again that a world which constantly emphasizes the sanctity of the individual and his liberation through organization is probably as conscious of the line of status and authority as any other group. Perhaps, because of the frequent pattern of sudden vaulting into power, many unionists were more conscious of status, as the *nouveaux riches* are traditionally more aware of their money than old, established families which have handled wealth for generations. I also learned that many of my radical friends who were so constantly in the habit of extolling the masses were most at home in a hierarchical structure far removed from the masses. The responses of men who are called upon to put their professions into practice are often strongly similar, be those men from the church, the union, or the university.

The Art of Association

There are two main political parties in the United States, as in England. These parties are voted in or out at elections, and during campaigns spokesmen of each exaggerate the differences between them. But the present-day Tories in England bear more resemblance, in actuality, to the American New Deal than to the Republican party. The Tories can afford to yield power to the opposition because their area of agreement with the opposition is wider than the area of disagreement. With the Republican and Democratic parties the area of likeness is perhaps even larger.

As we have seen, a modern democracy is a society of diffused power, a compensatory state, a state in which *majority rule* has come to mean something far more complex than the extension of universal suffrage to all members of the society. In this state, political power is diffused throughout an intricate system of wards, city machines, national bureaucracies, and hundreds of special interest groups; economic power may be closely allied with political power in this system, or it may be independent of it. (Charles Wilson, of General Motors, can afford to make such publicly outraging statements as "What is good for General Motors is good for the country" because, although he is at present part of the Republican political administration, he is also, as president of General Motors, independent of it.)

In such a state, "The People" may now be aligned with a majority, now with a minority. The minorities may represent outvoted groups, powerful special interest groups, or controlling—and controlled—leadership groups.

The English, without a formally written constitution, have developed and maintained for several centuries one of the most complex—and by parliamentary standards—one of the most exemplary of governments. The French have had written constitutions too numerous to mention, and have invented theories of government superb for close reasoning and succinct analysis, while at the same time maintaining—both before and after the French Revolution—a series of notoriously chaotic governmental structures. The Americans go on revering the Constitution with which they began, glibly ignoring its outdated elements, and happily continuing to play practical politics without much reference to abstract constitutional principles at all.

Americans are today perhaps the most practiced people in the world in what Alexis de Tocqueville, writing of them in 1835, called "the art of association." De Tocqueville had some reservations about "the unrestrained liberty of association for political purposes," which he considered to be "the last degree of liberty which a people is fit for," because "if it does not throw them into anarchy, it perpetually brings them, as it were, to the verge of it." However, he observed further that Americans never seemed to go in for revolutions because they were too busy making money:

> When you see the Americans freely and constantly forming associations for the purpose of promoting some political principle, of raising one man to the head of affairs, or of wresting power from another, you have some difficulty in understanding how men so independent do not constantly fall into the abuse of freedom. If, on the other hand, you survey the infinite number of trading companies in the United States . . . which the slightest revolution would throw into confusion, you will readily comprehend why people so well employed are by no means tempted to perturb the state or to destroy that public tranquillity by which they all profit.[2]

Men who have a positive stake in the society are eager to maintain what Havighurst has labeled "social cohesion." De Tocqueville saw Americans cementing social cohesion and learning their political footwork through what he called "civil associations."

> Certain men happen to have a common interest in some concern; either a commercial undertaking is to be managed, or some speculation in manufacture to be tried; they meet, they combine, and thus, by degrees, they become familiar with the principles of association. The greater the multiplicity of small affairs, the more do men, even without knowing it, acquire facility in prosecuting great undertakings in common.[3]

The American genius is to a large extent organizational; it is practical, wary, hard-headed; much like that Roman genius which once organized the ancient world into "civil" and political associations. The American believes that a large number of men can get more through organization than one man or a handful of men. It had to be Americans who would develop the idea of "group dynamics" in order to describe the inner workings of those multifold political and civil associations which they are busy setting up, and then abandoning in order to set up more.

The Auto Workers—Example of Trade Union Democracy

What are the inner workings of this "multiplicity of small affairs" which teach men how to govern the state? The United Automobile Workers of America, for example, would be an instance of that subtle and often baffling relationship between leader and follower under the omnipresent aegis of the Organization. "These proposals have been drafted," say the leaders. "Our people have pushed us to adopt these proposals; the Organization must ratify them." Meanwhile, the worker is saying: "These proposals have been drafted by the leaders; the Organization has ratified them. We must either adopt them or defy the Organization." The question, of course, seems obvious: what or who is the Organization? Can it survive without leaders, without workers? Does it go on despite leaders, despite workers?

Now the present leadership of the Auto Workers is perhaps as intelligent and honest a body of staff members as can be found in any organization anywhere. But all intelligent and honest leadership—perhaps more than other kinds—is faced with the continual possibility of alienation from the people whom it leads and to whom it is responsible. Workers, like other people, secretly resent being led, and in sensitive and cunning fashion, therefore, they often fabricate unreal desires for the pleasure and approval of their leaders, or they may keep back their real feelings in order to confuse or placate their leaders. The worker is temperamental; he is likely to crucify his leaders in the morning and re-instate them in the evening. The workers are also mistrustful; they feel that the leadership is likely at any given time to "put something over" on them; the leaders, in their turn, feel that the workers are unreasonable if not incalculable. On certain appointed nights I have seen workers and leaders get together to drink in rowdy truce; and at that time I have observed that everyone pretends to have only the most easily understood desires. The workers pretend to be what they think the leaders want them to be; and the leaders pretend to be what they think the workers want *them* to be, for sometimes they want to feel "one with the worker" very badly.

This oneness is difficult to achieve even if the leadership does not happen to differ from its followers in socioeconomic origin. Oneness is difficult to achieve because the very possibilities of power and the weight of responsibility automatically set the leader apart. The absolute ruler may be more subject to the temptations and terrors of power than the modern labor leader; but I think that this is a difference of degree rather than of kind. Absolute rule carries with it the possibility of inhuman excess, and therefore of insanity; Nero is a legendary figure precisely because he succumbed to the frantic fears inherent in his isolation from other men; Peter the Great and Catherine the Great led personal lives heavily rouged with calculated madness. Charles V, Emperor of the Holy Roman Empire, who took the responsibilities of power and worked at them conscientiously, voluntarily resigned both power and responsibility to spend his last years in a monastery. The argument that Henry Adams gives us for a well-trained and functioning aristocracy was the fact that "power in the hands of friends is an advantage . . . no mind is so well-balanced as to bear the strain of seizing unlimited force without habit or knowledge of it. . . . The effect of unlimited power on limited minds is worth noting in Presidents because it must represent the same process in society, and the power of self-control must have limit somewhere in face of the control of the infinite."[4]

Honest and intelligent democratic leadership (which we have shown exemplified in the Auto Workers) is not faced with "control of the infinite," but is faced certainly with the problem of both real and imagined isolation. Like the minister's son in a small town, the leader is expected to be more human than other people's children in some respects, and in other respects not human at all. Thus leaders and followers seek out Oneness in the concept of the Organization, that mythical monster which is bigger than both of them, and which technically has the right to shed either of them like old skins, or to use either of them for its own, larger purposes. The Organization does not exist, except on paper and in the minds of its members, but the idea of the Organization is the Higher Good for which the leaders initiate action, upon which the workers act, and the name which the dissident factions invoke.

Now the union itself, as an organization, is a faction upon the national scene; within the union are numberless fratricidal groups which in miniature fashion represent the larger national factional struggles. In miniature fashion, too, these factional struggles within the union organization show the difficulties of minority-majority relationships within a technically democratic super-structure. For example, Local 600, UAW-CIO, constitutes a powerful dissident faction within the Auto Workers. It is powerful because it is the largest union local in the world (over 50,000 members) and because its membership is active and self-aware. In March of 1953 when the Auto Workers held their annual convention at Atlantic City, the adoption of the Guaranteed Annual Wage plan was officially proposed by the majority leadership of the union, and officially opposed by the dissident leadership of Local 600. Local 600 had its own alternative to the Guaranteed Annual Wage, the "30-40" plan (thirty hours work for forty hours pay).

On the floor of the convention hall, one of Local 600's leaders, Carl Stellato, delivered a brief outline of the 30-40 plan. (Stellato, generally looked upon as the head of the anti-Reuther forces in the UAW, was described to me by one of his brothers in Local 600, as a man who allegedly "does everything just enough—you know what I mean? He drinks—but just enough; talks—but just enough, never too much; smokes—but just enough. He's shrewd; his wife is shrewd like that; and his kids are shrewd.")

In his presentation of the 30-40 plan, Stellato said:

I would like to refresh your memory, Brother Reuther, to an article that appeared in the New York Times Magazine on August 26, 1944—"A 30-Hour Week After the War?"

"Yes, says Walter Reuther of the Auto Workers; No, say Eric Johnston and Henry J. Kaiser."

In 1947, in your opening remarks to that Convention, after you had been president for one year, you tore Wilson to pieces, and rightfully so, because he was talking of a 45-hour week with no overtime. You insisted we go to bat for a 30-hour week with 40 hours' pay.

The debate raged back and forth. Majority spokesmen charged that the 30-40 proposal was a Communist bloc "to restrict production"; Local 600 leaders returned that Guaranteed Annual Wage would place "a knife in the back of our brothers in the rubber, longshore, and building industries. They have the six-hour day, 30-hour week, with overtime rates beyond those hours."

Emil Mazey, Secretary-Treasurer of the UAW, acted the role of the middle-of-the-roader, the pacifying agent:

Nobody here is arguing against the merits of the 30-hour week; the whole argument is on the basis of timing. I think if we view all of the arguments and the obstacles and the problems that we have now that you will find it just doesn't make sense.

If between now and 1955 we should have a shift in the development of our economy where a question of the 30-hour week with 40-hour pay might be the thing that we ought to do at that time, we have plenty of opportunity of raising the question in our '55 Convention and taking a look at this entire matter.

It was, however, Walter Reuther who clinched the matter —on the basis of majority rule:

We went to Washington. We had 600 delegates at the Defense Unemployment Conference. We had two hours of debate on these resolutions of the 30-hour week, and when the vote was taken there were 587 votes against the 30-hour week and 13 votes for the 30-hour week, and the next issue of FORD FACTS (Local 600 newspaper) said that we sold the membership down the river; that it was a handpicked conference.

The real issue here is not: are you an honest trade unionist? You can believe in the 30-hour week today or tomorrow and you can be as honest as anybody else.

The real issue involves majority rule. I ask the fellows from Local 600 who exercise the right of democratic expression in this Convention to exercise the right to express their point of view but when the Convention has spoken and the will of the majority has been made clear, I say if you want the rights and privileges you have got to accept the responsibility to *go back home and carry out the will of the majority.* . . .

Every time we have to dissipate our time and our energy and our strength with these internal squabbles, we are weakening our Union and I say to this small group of brothers: Put the Union first and you will have no trouble with anybody of our family.[5]

Thus the last, the final, appeal was made in the name of the Organization. The leaders of the majority position refuted the claims of the 30-40 men on the grounds that it would be impossible to negotiate the plan with any company in the country, and that it would be suicidal to send workers out on strike for provisions which are nonnegotiable. Presumably, following the adoption of the

Guaranteed Wage resolution, the UAW family closed ranks in order to carry out the majority rule decision. For at this point, labor would find itself talking to management, and Walter Reuther was paraphrasing another man when he said "Put the Union first. . . . " (A house divided against itself cannot stand.)

In reality, of course, all houses are divided on a factional basis; the trouble starts when a house is almost equally divided against itself, so that there is not a large enough group to constitute a ruling majority. And management, talking to labor on the annual wage (or any other issue), speaks words and gets words spoken back in at least a partial vacuum: for it is not so much labor and management talking to each other as both of them addressing the American public, which sometimes hears and sometimes doesn't. The actual pushing through of a series of modified annual wage plans during the spring of 1955 was accomplished not only through negotiations between Reuther men and General Motors men; it was accomplished through a public relations drive (radio, newspapers, education) which went on previous to and concomitant with the actual period of negotiation. In the end, Carl Stellato's opposition group was vindicated. Describing their "historic new contracts," an article in the UAW-CIO periodical, AMMUNITION, states:

> Meanwhile, the union's next major bargaining goal already has been mapped by convention resolution.
>
> It will be the shorter work week.[6]

Public Opinion and the Public

Perhaps this illustration will serve to make clear that a democratic state can be thought of only as a society of diverse publics. In modern-day America we must visualize publics which are so interrelated, so overlapping, and so diverse as to make the frightening and comforting term "Public Opinion" seem almost impossible to define. Public Opinion is molded by all kinds of leadership—including advertising agents (public taste), leaders of industry (consumption), newspaper reporters and editors, schoolteachers, preachers, politicians, some kinds of businessmen, leaders of labor, civic leaders. Harriet Beecher Stowe may certainly have inflamed antislavery opinion with *Uncle Tom's Cabin;* but it is difficult to gauge her influence in so far as antislavery opinion had already been well formed before the appearance of the Beecher book, and was ripe for inflammation.

At the same time that it is molded, however, Public Opinion also creates the attitudes of its ostensible leaders. For example, everyone in Chicago knows that Public Opinion is a fickle thing; nevertheless, all corrupt officials and gangsters in Chicago are terrified of It, because when It rises in Its wrath (which It has been known to do following some particularly shocking murder or scandal), It can sweep all before it. The sweeping is a temporary thing, however, and this is why

Public Opinion is known to be fickle. Public Opinion in this sense might be described as a number of specific publics (taste, consumption, belief, ethnic and social groupings) which form a common consensus in certain areas relating to public and private morality (or, if not morality, at least convention). Moviemakers in this country (who have long been thought of as prime molders of public opinion) are very deeply influenced in their production by what they think the public wants. Public Opinion for people who make their living out of it seems incalculable. It may criticize its ostensible leaders for doing precisely those things which It permits itself to do. It is incalculable because no amount of pushing and priming is necessarily going to make It move on issues; whereas a sudden, an unforeseen, an inflammatory incident will do so.

Public Opinion in this sense, then, is a massive group —cutting across all other special interest groups—which is capable of acting in concert on certain violations of basic beliefs. And even under the most absolute kind of government, public opinion is important. "I conclude," says that shrewd observer, Machiavelli, "that a prince need trouble little about conspiracies when the people are well disposed, but when they are hostile and hold him in hatred, then he must fear everything and everybody. Well-ordered states and wise princes have studied diligently not to drive the nobles to desperation, and to satisfy the populace and keep it contented, for this is one of the most important matters that a prince has to deal with."[7]

The special interest groups, meanwhile, constitute the specific publics which make up the larger It. Everywhere, in every time, rulers have been in danger of being thrown out of power by the military, by the nobility, by invasions—or by the populace. All rulers have had to deal with power blocs within the body politic (the house divided many times over against itself). All intelligent rulers have been occupied in keeping a balance of power between competing groups.

Machiavelli goes on:

> Whence it may be seen that hatred is gained by good works as by evil, and therefore . . . a prince who wishes to maintain the state is often forced to do evil, for when that party, whether populace, soldiery, or nobles, *whichever it be that you consider necessary to you for keeping your position*, is corrupt, you must follow its humor and satisfy it, and in that case good works will be inimical to you. . . . Marcus, Pertinax, and Alexander, being all of modest life, lovers of justice, enemies of cruelty, humane and benign, all came to a sad end except Marcus. Marcus (the philosopher) alone lived and died in honor, because he succeeded to the empire by hereditary right and did not owe it either to the soldiers or to the people; besides which, possessing virtues which made him revered, he kept both parties in their place as long as he lived and was never either hated or despised.[8]

All states, in the terms with which Machiavelli deals, are made up of lobbies. But as we have seen in a foregoing chapter, the democratic state is made up of lobbies and something plus lobbies. That something more is not just public opinion (for public opinion has always counted for something), but rather, public opinion under law. In democratic theory, the majority will should be able to create or revoke any law it so desires; in democratic practice lobby groups of one kind or another work to influence the majority will, and lawyers work either to twist or to interpret it. In democratic theory, the law stands above all men and is the equalizer of all men; in democratic practice, judges can be bought, lawyers can be bribed, and legislators can be influenced by any special interest group which has enough money and energy to throw into the task.

The history of lobbying in America is, in effect, the history of American legislation. . . . Every reader of history knows that hirelings of every interest—railroads, manufacturers, bankers, farmers—have haunted the lobbies of every Congress, sometimes with the most corrupt intent and sometimes to press for the passage of laws which posterity has found good. . . . In the days of the great debate over the form of government to be set up in the newly independent nation neither the word "lobby" nor the word "lobbyist" had been invented (except as an architectural term). But James Madison, at least, was well aware of the dangerous potentialities of the pressure group, as his famous *Federalist* (No. 10) makes clear. Substitute the word "lobby" for "faction" in its most widely quoted passage and his warning is seen to have lost little potency over the years:

"By faction," he wrote, "I understand a number of citizens, whether amounting to a majority or a minority of the whole, who are united and actuated by some common impulse of passion, or of interest, adverse to the rights of other citizens, or the permanent and aggregate interests of the community."[9]

Later, one of the most powerful and influential of the lobbies, the prohibitionists, succeeded in pushing through Congress the "medieval idea of sumptuary legislation governing private conduct by fiat of law."[10] In 1913 the Webb-Kenyon prohibition act was passed, and in 1917 upheld by the Supreme Court. When the Eighteenth Amendment (prohibiting sale or use of intoxicating liquors) became part of the Constitution of the United States, the speakeasy era was officially begun. Great fortunes were made through the sale of bootleg liquors, and everybody broke the law with an impunity which makes the memory of the 1920's ring yet with loud and scandalous gaiety. When it was finally agreed upon that prohibition was one of the most foolish pieces of legislation ever put through Congress, the Eighteenth Amendment was repealed.

The prohibitionists were the first organized minority to show the way to make use of this technique on a national scale. Since then we have learned that what seems like a "nationwide movement of public opinion" is far too often nothing more than the synthetic creation of lobbyists and propagandists for special interests working against the national welfare for the sometimes open, but more often hidden, purpose of their employers.[11]

By 1925 the American Legion had assumed enormous importance as a lobby in Washington. One of the Legion's star lobbyists, John Thomas Taylor, boasted that he had personally written some 1500 to 2000 bills during a stretch of ten years, and that a good number of these bills had become law. At an annual convention of the Legion, the organization's legislative committee once laid down its attitude toward lobbying:

> It must be recognized that . . . Congress does not lead in settling questions of public, political, or economic policy. . . . Legislation is literally made outside the halls of Congress by groups of persons interested in legislation, mainly with economic motives; and the deliberative process within Congress constitutes a sort of formal ratification.[12]

In 1946, lobbying was legalized, but in some manner restrained, by the Regulation of Lobbying Act which provided that all lobbying groups make known the source of their funds and the identification of their particular interest.

Lobbying in a Democracy

The rise and success of lobbying brings to light again the basic problem of majority rule in a democratic country. The problem is one not merely of getting to the people, but of providing the people with a means and a way to get to their representatives. "Nobody," said Walter Reuther in 1948, "can guarantee the labor vote!" On another level this means that nobody—not even the most skilled lobbyist—can guarantee what the people will do next. The huge forces of the press and corporative interests which guaranteed and predicted the election of Dewey to the Presidency in 1948 ate cold turkey; powerful as they were, even they could not guarantee the vote. We have pointed out the ever-present threat of hiatus between Worker and Leader; the same threat exists to an even greater degree in the relationship between Leaders and People.

Thus, both management and labor appeal to Public Opinion (and on another level, to Law) as the final arbiter between them. The relationship between these two concepts—Law and the People—might best be understood if we take an example of Law being passed to protect "our" side as against Opinion on "their" side. I refer to the recent Supreme Court decision outlawing segregation of Negroes and white people in schools all over the nation. In other words, in terms of Southern public opinion, the law represented a minority liberal viewpoint passed, if you will, on the basis of expediency; for one reason given for the law was that its enactment would proclaim to the whole world that America would officially treat its white and nonwhite citizens as equal under the law. (And those who argued for the expediency above and beyond the moral referred to *the world* in terms of the Asiatic world, so important to American foreign policy. In that sense, Asiatic Public Opinion might be said to have won out—by sheer numerical and economic importance—over Southern white American public opinion.)

Lobbying, then, and the whole process which it represents—the minority working actively to influence the majority—can be worked for either good or evil ends, or for results which are a mixture of good and evil. The Taft-Hartley Act, to take another example, exemplified an issue on which unions and employers have sought to influence public opinion and government action in their behalf. By employers it was represented as a bill to "free" labor, to preserve the worker's right of individual choice. Organized labor fought Taft-Hartley as a bill which, if put into practice, would "enslave" labor. Its enactment represented the triumph in Congress of its supporters, but not necessarily a final triumph. It remains an issue, and both groups are still hard at work convincing the public that it is a "good" or a "bad" piece of legislation. At the last national political convention time (1952), both parties considered it, both parties heard arguments by the interested groups, and both parties gave it recognition as an issue in their platforms. Candidates find it necessary to take positions on the issue, and each takes what he hopes will be the most popular position. His position, he argues, is *consistent with the public interest*; his opponent's position is inimical to the public interest.

The difference between business, labor, and agriculture—to mention three main pressure groups on the

American scene—appears in their contrasting definitions of the *public interest* and in their different notions about the way in which it is best advanced. Organized labor believes that it is in the public interest to lift the level of living for all by lifting the level of purchasing power of the organized workers, and to organize the unorganized so that they may have similar privileges. They believe that there is much to be done as long as income is presently so distributed (1950 census) that the lowest 20 per cent of income recipients in America receive 3 per cent of the total money income, whereas the highest 20 per cent receive 47 per cent. Other pressure groups define the public interest differently. The farmer argues that agriculture is the backbone of the nation. Business insists that the nation's economic strength is dependent on the creation of jobs by the entrepreneur and by his consistent expansion of capital investment, produced through work and savings.

The lobbying activities stemming from these diverse points of view take several forms. Most commonly, lobbying provides a channel for communicating public opinion and the interests of special groups to legislators. Both law and management interview legislators and appear before legislative committees to give information on pending bills. An examination of the records of committee hearings over the past several decades shows an increasing representation of labor in these hearings. Moreover, labor now comes supplied with its own ex-

perts—lawyers, economists, statisticians, and the like—
to match the experts who testify for business groups.

A second type of lobbying, which stresses the giving
or withholding of support depending upon the yes or no
of the legislator, is carried on differently by the two
groups. Organized labor—like the American Legion and
any other well-organized lobby group—judges senators
and representatives by their voting records in committee
and by roll call on so-called labor bills. If the legislator
fails to measure up to expectations, he is threatened with
the withdrawal of support by labor's voting bloc.

In reality, labor—even organized labor—does not
vote as a bloc, and though the leaders may influence its
vote, they cannot, as Walter Reuther admitted, control
it or deliver it. Almost one-third of all families in
America are "labor union" families, but union members
constitute one of the groups in the population with a
low voter-turnout ratio. Moreover, in the presidential
election of 1952, one out of three union members voted
for the Republican candidate despite the recommenda-
tions by top leaders to support the Democratic candidate.
Nevertheless, unions do organize political action committees, and they do work to get out the vote; they represent a formidable number, and their voting strength
cannot be lightly dismissed.

Employers and business groups can point to no such
voting group, but they have a particular advantage
which not even a united labor organization can balance.

Industry groups, in short, can offer or withhold another kind of support than political pull. The great game of politics in the United States is an expensive one. The man of average income cannot play it, for the man of average income is too dependent upon contributions for the cost of his election, and it is here, as was so clearly indicated in the hearings on the Taft campaign, that big money talks. In fact, it often talks for men of independent fortune, corporation executives, or the corporation lawyers who represent them.

The Fix and the Squeeze

The fix and the squeeze, which are characteristics of the third and most destructive type of lobbying, also require sizable expenditure. It is this kind of political activity which undermines public morals and destroys public confidence. In a complex society such as ours, where economic advantage is avidly sought, more and more individuals and organizations look to government as a means of engineering this advantage—through grants-in-aid, government contracts, price supports, tax exemption, and the like. In the confusion which is Capitol Hill, the uninitiated seek the help of the initiated, and money and liquor flow to bridge the gaps of calculated reason. Both the venal and the unsophisticated live in a world of influence. Both agree that the only way to get things done in Washington is through someone else and that "after all, the halls of Congress are too large and the mazes of the Pentagon too complex for the average person to comprehend." The danger stemming from such a philosophy is that the fix and the squeeze may become so firmly institutionalized in our culture (as in China) that they will threaten the very basis of our democratic process; for in the last analysis the integrity of the law and the stability of our institutions is dependent upon the integrity of the men who administer them.

The fact that employer groups have more money gives them a decided advantage in employing the mass media. The full-page ad and the radio speech of the company executive are standard operating procedures for business factions. But these are expensive procedures, and those persons who pick up the checks in the labor movement know that they cannot compete with the great business organizations in these areas. Although the public-service responsibility of the radio stations compels them to give time for the discussions of public issues, that time is often given when listeners are few. Further, as was discovered in 1946 during the steelworkers' and others' strikes, the purchase of too much space and time by unions to tell their story may have a negative effect. The public asks how, if the workers are as hard up as they claim, their unions can afford such big expenditures for radio time and ads.

There are other important reasons why the mass media lend themselves more readily to use by employer groups than to use by organized labor. Employer groups have no large membership base to which they can appeal and which, in turn, will reach others outside their groups. They must use these media to reach, if only at a superficial level, the public. Though the public is undoubtedly influenced to some extent, there is good reason to believe that under many circumstances the mass appeal falls flat. From 1936 on, 90 to 95 per cent of the American press opposed Franklin Roosevelt. Americans are a very literate people; nevertheless, they elected Roosevelt to the office of President for four terms.

It is generally true that genuine education—or genuine indoctrination, if you will—proceeding through the exchange of ideas in person-to-person relationships, repeatedly has triumphed over the mass-media exchange. In 1944, CIO-PAC put out a minimum of 40 million pieces of literature to help re-elect Franklin Roosevelt. The AFL during the same year put out little or no literature. On the basis of studies made since the election, it can be stated that approximately 71 per cent of the registered CIO voters went Democratic, while about 68 per cent of the registered AFL voters cast Democratic ballots. Forty million pieces of literature and a three per cent difference in the voting pattern!

The Public Resolves

Thus it comes about that labor and management—or any two opposing groups—talk to each other against a background screen of public opinion. There results a kind of ambivalence. Union leaders must make a vigorous effort to secure what their membership demands, yet these demands must be reasonable if the public support is to be gained. Similarly, company executives may find themselves reporting to their stockholders and investors that under their management, profits are at a record level, while at the same time resisting workers' demands for wage increases in order to protect those profits, and with a third voice appealing to the public on grounds that the workers' demands are unreasonable. The public-relations program is as much concerned with keeping the membership happy, as it is with influencing public opinion by convincing the larger population that the group is behaving in accord with the general public interest. Because this is true, there arises the interesting phenomenon of both parties to industrial conflict identifying their organizational aims with human and national welfare. Business does not advertise that it is in business to make profits. Rather, it "makes possible the employment of hundreds of thousands"; it provides "the dependable efficient . . . service so essential to the economic well-being and military strength of the nation."

The center of the CIO's public relations program was at one time a mailing list made up of some 120,000 people from all over the United States. This list was broken up into some fifty-two categories consisting of teachers, ministers, political scientists, educators, reporters, radio announcers, organization heads, and so on (groups responsible for segments of diffused power). These people were mailed a consistent flow of literature interpreting the CIO position on various issues. In time of crisis—strikes and otherwise—the reasons for the CIO's direct action were accompanied by a personal letter attempting to identify the reader's interest with that of the CIO. Whenever replies to the literature were received from interested parties, their names were put on cards and classified according to states and Congressional districts. It was this list which became the nucleus of much of PAC when labor went into politics full tilt in 1944. The philosophy behind such a mode of organization was clear-cut and previously defined—that person-to-person relations are more important in influencing opinion than a barrage of propaganda which can provide only the initial contact for establishing such personal relationships.

One of the most pertinent facts about our society in the light of this kind of analysis is that the lobby or the pressure group serves a function. At the ideal level of democratic centralization of power, these lobby groups should come from all areas of society. On the real level they do not. The majority of voluntary organization groups in the country, the majority of independent citizens' groups, operate on very little money and under the difficulty of finding people who will donate time and energy to keep them functioning. The apathy of public opinion on most issues is well-founded. The individual citizen feels, and with some validity, that he cannot change the system by himself. He feels that he cannot do much about the system through a voluntary organization which has no real power-base. The individual knows that as the conflicting economic groups grow larger and more powerful, more and more of the decisions which affect him are made by top-level experts and politicians. As long as this trend continues, people will feel that they can do little or nothing to affect their own destiny. And as long as people feel this way, the trend toward centralization of power in the United States will continue.

The people are apathetic because the metallic dissemination of mass-media opinions has ceased to stir them up. In a more and more depersonalized society, they come to feel a little less human, far more a helpless prey of impersonal forces and driving necessities. The vicious circle never ends until an individual or a group of individuals cuts through to the core of the dilemma and under the influence of a strong conviction, personalizes politics once again.

The Motives of the Governing

It is apparent that one of the basic problems of all governments is to insure that men who have power will not grow corrupt, negligent, and inefficient in the wielding of it. This is sometimes accomplished by displacing men from power and putting other men in their place (and a democratic society provides for the orderly and periodical working of this process); sometimes it is accomplished by grooming men for power, rearing them for the exercise of it. This is the solution which Plato suggested in *The Republic*; it is the solution which has been used from time to time by aristocratic societies. Cardinal Richelieu and Winston Churchill are two outstanding examples of men who were born, groomed, reared, and prepared for power; they *belonged* there; they could have little doubt as to their fitness to wield power. In this way, aristocratic societies are not so outmoded as, on the first glance of the democrat, they may seem. It is only when the aristocracy ceases to perform its function, ceases to carry out the responsibilities with which it is charged, that they become poor inane appendages only fit for replacement.

As we have seen, the people who controlled the original thirteen colonies were an aristocratic minority; but all hope of aristocratic rule became invalid after the election of Andrew Jackson to the presidency in 1828. The election of Jackson marked the final triumph of the Yankee over the Puritan, for in the New England beginnings the Yankee and the Puritan had struggled for dominance,

> . . . in an interweaving of idealism and economics—by the substantial body of thought and customs and institutions brought from the old home, slowly modified by new ways of

life developing under the silent pressure of a freer environment.

From these sources emerged the two chief classes of New England: the yeomanry, a body of democratic freeholders who constituted the rank and file of the people, and the gentry, a group of capable merchants who dominated the commonwealth from early days to the rise of industrialism. And it was the interweaving of the aims and purposes of these acquisitive yeoman and gentry—harmonious for the most part on the surface, yet driving in different directions —with the ideal of a theocracy and the inhibitions of Puritan dogma, that constitutes the pattern of life to be dealt with here. The Puritan and the Yankee were the two halves of the New England whole. . . . The Puritan was a contribution to the old world, created by the rugged idealism of the English Reformation; the Yankee was a product of native conditions, created by a practical economics.[13]

Much of indigenous American radicalism in the United States—from William Jennings Bryan and the Populists through Henry Wallace—can be traced to the continuing revolt of the Yankee against the Puritan, the frontiersman against the political control of the East, the agrarian against the economic control of the city.

Andrew Jackson himself was not only the symbol of broadening suffrage and an expanding economy; he was a living denial of the whole Puritan theocratic structure, the idea that "ordinary mortals needed instruction, guidance, perhaps even coercion by their enlightened and duly designated leaders." It was because of Jackson, and all the forces which Jackson represented, that Henry

Adams—grandson of John Quincy and great-grandson of John Adams—was to lament long and eloquently that he was born too late to take that part in honorable statesmanship which by training, birthright, family tradition, and intelligence, he had been created for. His education, indeed, fitted him for nothing but the aristocratic sidelines and backwaters in a country which was busy electing uneducated men on horseback to the presidency. "America had no use for Adams because he was eighteenth century, and yet it worshipped Ulysses Grant because he was archaic. . . ."[14]

Adams studied men like Grant and Garibaldi, seeing them as "forces of nature" which expressed the blind will of the majority and were themselves blind, with strange, untutored, sphinxlike peasant minds, but with energy (and energy is always admirable, even when its direction is unclear). He identified power with the personalities which wielded it and the forces behind personality which permitted its realization in fact. Adams' most fascinating problem was the relationship between power and morality.

> He (Adams) knew well enough all that was to be said for the gold standard as economy, but he had never in his life taken politics for a pursuit of economy. . . . From early childhood his moral principles had struggled blindly with his interests, but he was certain of one law which ruled all others—*masses of men invariably follow interests in deciding morals*. Morality is a private and costly luxury. . . . He had, in a halfhearted way, struggled all his life against State

Street, banks, capitalism altogether, as he knew it in old
England or New England. . . . [15]

Many years later, an indirect descendant of the Henry
Adams tradition, Franklin D. Roosevelt, was to be called
—with great irony—"a class traitor." But Roosevelt's
struggle against State Street and the banks was confined
within a strict arena in which the superior man was he
who could juggle all the existing forces in American
society in at least a partially harmonious cacophony.

Since Adams never entered politics, he made daring
and unsparing use of his function as a critic, and an outsider. But while other, later critics of the American political and economic scene—such as Lincoln Steffens—
would turn momentarily toward early Russian Bolshevism or toward the corporate state of Mussolini, Adams
could find no such way out in his war with finance-
capitalism. He explains his inability to become a Marxist with tongue in cheek, as a personal flaw.

By rights (Adams) should have been also a Marxist, but
some narrow trait in the New England nature seemed to
blight socialism, and he tried in vain to make himself a convert.[16]

Nevertheless, he came to describe Karl Marx and
Auguste Comte as the "two writers of his time who most
influenced his thought." On his first trip to England,
Adams described his journey through Birmingham and
the Black District, what he calls "the revelation of an
unknown society of the pit," followed by a "sense of

unknown horror," and the later realization that "Karl
Marx was standing there waiting for him, and sooner or
later the process of education would have to deal with
Karl Marx more than with Professor Bowen of Harvard
College or his Satanic free-trade majesty, John Stuart
Mill."[17]

Adams finally came to see American society as a
dynamo, and American politics as a game, a game which
had nothing to do with the more philosophic problems of
morality, of ends and means.

> In this game . . . there was nothing but the amusement of
> the pugilist or acrobat. . . . The work of domestic progress
> is done by masses of mechanical power . . . controlled by
> a score or two of individuals who have shown capacity to
> manage it. The work of internal government has become the
> task of controlling these men, who are socially as remote as
> heathen gods, alone worth knowing, but never known, and
> who could tell nothing of political value if one skinned them
> alive. Most of them have nothing to tell, but are forces as
> dumb as their dynamos, absorbed in the development or
> economy of power. . . . Modern politics is, at bottom, a
> struggle not of men, but of forces. The men become every
> year more and more creatures of force.[18]

In one sense, Henry Adams was the last Puritan battling
humorously and sadly against the arrayed forces of the
triumphant Yankee. In another sense, he was the aristocratic scion yearning for more grace and beauty in
American life, and more right to be individualist and
different; still more patently, he was the unconvinced

Marxist who believed stupidity (the nonscientific and unplanned management of history and economics) to be immoral. Still more significantly, he was the old-line democrat watching a Gargantuan nation becoming a dynamo without a soul—without even a political soul. Democracy is dead, mourned Adams, like the Constitution my fathers wrote. For what piece of paper, what declaration of rights, can stand against the purely impersonal forces of economic growth and aggrandizement? Those were the old rules.

One kind of criticism Adams left out—the anarchist kind. But Henry David Thoreau had spoken for that, and in his famous essay on Civil Disobedience declared that once and for all time there is no point in a government except as "an expedient by which man would fain succeed in letting one another alone. . . . Must the citizen, ever for a moment, or in the least degree, resign his conscience to the legislator? I cannot for an instant recognize that political organization as my government which is the slave's government also."[19]

Henry Adams, after all, was a Puritan in corrupt form. He yearned for morality, but he realized all the complications in the way of its fulfillment. Thoreau, alone and uncorrupted, brushed all such complicating factors aside. There is a higher morality, said Thoreau simply, which is above all Caesars and all constitutional majorities. It is the plain duty of a man to adhere to the higher law. No compromise is possible with the conscience.

Chapter 5

Saints and heroes are the true teachers of mankind.
—JACQUES MARITAIN

A Standard to which the Just Can Repair

THE trial and death of Socrates proved his own contention that the power—and seeming powerlessness—of a wise man could gain the whole world by appearing to lose it. The democratic world is a reasonable one, involving among other things, individual responsibility. It is also an ethical world in its belief that men are capable of making their own choices, of governing themselves.

The reader who learns in "The Affirmation" in this chapter something of Kermit Eby's family and religious background will gain some understanding of why he believes that the mature man is he who not only has ideals but is courageous enough to attempt their transmutation into reality.

The Ethic

Several hundred years ago, Thomas Hobbes described a world in which war is peace, aggression is defense, honor is power, and dishonor is poverty and ill-fortune:

So that in the first place, I put for a general inclination of all mankind, a perpetual and restless desire of power after power, that ceases only in death. And the cause of this, is not always that a man hopes for a more intensive delight, than he has already attained to; or that he cannot be content with a moderate power; but because he cannot assure the power and means to live well, which he has at present, without the acquisition of more. . . . Competition of riches, honor, command, or other power, inclines to contention, enmity, and war; because the way of one competitor, to the attaining of his desire, is to kill, subdue, supplant, or repel the other.[1]

The Hobbesian world lacks a certain imaginative quality; it differs from the real world in one major aspect. In the real world men thirst after righteousness as well as after power. "Nor does it alter the case of honor," Hobbes states, "whether an action (so it be great and difficult, and consequently a sign of much power) be just or unjust; for honor consists only in the opinion of power."[2]

There was little room in the Hobbesian universe for a man like Socrates, who would persuade his followers "to seek virtue and wisdom before he looks to his private interests." Hobbes tells us that power wins all things; Socrates, that the superior power (and seeming powerlessness) of a single wise man could gain the whole world by appearing to lose it. Socrates proved his contention in much the same manner as Christ, by yielding up his own life for the sake of the thesis. The trial of

Socrates became the classic case of the quarrel between society and its gods and the individual and his ethic. The Athenians seem almost to have deliberately planned and executed their classic problem, and to have left the resolution open to all mankind and to all succeeding generations.

The case was classic, too, because there was almost no politics involved in it. On trial was the purity of one man; in question was one teacher's right to speak. In one sense Socrates was tried for his nonpartisanship, his skepticism rather than his adherence to a fixed idea. The Athenians gave him every possibility to state his case, and to have the case recorded by loving disciples (who were allowed to weep over him in death, and to write of him fondly after his death). In brief, these people chose a well-born Athenian, a member of the tribe of Antiochis, a man regarded by many as the wisest among them, and they accorded him singular honors: fame, the reputation of greatness, powerful enemies and powerful friends, an honorable death by hemlock—and finally, immortality.

For some reason the case of Socrates has been transmitted to us on this intellectual plane. The emotion at the trial may have run high, but it does not seem to have been the kind of emotion which is engendered by a man who is thought to have dishonored the name of *our women*, desecrated *our country*, outraged *our sacred honor*, or blasphemed *our gods*. Nor does it seem to have been the trial of a man who is seriously thought to have endangered the state.

Indeed, there was little trace of the civil disobedience idea in the Socratic argument. This man had fought bravely for Athens on the battlefield; he had carried out public responsibilities; he was the respected member of a community; he had led a life which would bear close examination.

It was never really proved that Socrates *was* a political or moral dissident; it was proved only that he *reserved the right to dissent,* and to examine all ideas in the light of reason, in the light of logic.

Simply to prove his logic, then, Socrates had to die. He was given the alternative of exile, and rejected it. Speaking to somewhat reasonable men, he presented his reasonable argument:

> Men of Athens, I honor and love you; but I shall obey God rather than you, and while I have life and strength, I shall never cease from the practice and teaching of philosophy, exhorting anyone whom I meet. . . . For I am certain, O men of Athens, that if I had engaged in politics, I should have perished long ago . . . for the truth is, that no man who goes to war with you or any other multitude, honestly striving against the many lawless and unrighteous deeds which are done in a state, will save his life; he who will fight for the right, if he would live in even for a brief space, must have a private station and not a public one. . . . The only office of state which I ever held, O men of Athens, was that of senator; the tribe Antiochis, which is my tribe, had the presidency at the trial of the generals who had not taken up the bodies of the slain after the battle of Arginusae; and you proposed to try them in a body, contrary to law, as you

all thought afterwards; but at the time I was the only one of the Prytanes who was opposed to illegality, and I gave my vote against you; and when the orators threatened to impeach and arrest me, *and you called and shouted, I made up my mind that I would run the risk, having law and justice with me,* rather than take part in your injustice because I feared imprisonment and death. This happened in the days of the democracy. . . . Now do you really imagine that I could have survived all these years, if I had led a public life, supposing that like a good man, I had always maintained the right and had made justice, as I ought, the first thing?[3]

Socrates was one of those Happy Few who died—not for a cause, not for a political party, not for a nation nor yet for an ideology—but for the simple and not easily granted right to examine in the interests of speculative philosophy, in the interests of a larger truth. Too reasonable to have been a martyr, Socrates argued that perhaps death is the greatest good man can know, since in any case man does not know what death is. There is a great deal of difference between the death of a Socrates (a man standing alone, without church and without ideology and demanding the right to reason free of community restraint), and the death of the Christian martyrs who, collectively and in terms of power, fatally threatened the still "partially well-ordered world of Marcus Aurelius."

. . . A better Christian in all but the dogmatic sense of the word than almost any of the ostensibly Christian sovereigns

who have since reigned [Marcus Aurelius] persecuted Christianity. . . . Existing society he knew to be in a deplorable
condition, but such as it was, he saw, or thought he saw,
*that it was held together, and prevented from being made
worse by belief and reverence in the received divinities.* As a
ruler of mankind, he deemed it his duty not to suffer society
to fall to pieces. . . . The new religion openly aimed at dis-
solving these ties; unless, therefore, it was his duty to adopt
that religion, it seemed to be his duty to put it down.[4]

When we deal with motives as complicated as those of
Marcus Aurelius, or with historical and ideological
trends as complex as those which resulted in the death
of Socrates, it becomes obvious that we must look beyond
the intricacies of politics in the search for a standard to
which the just can repair. We know that much blood has
been spilled from the purest of motives and under the
guidance of the most impeccable of men. We know that
the Lawgiver has always been deep in a running feud
with the Prophet, and that the Lawgiver is often characterized by rigid and inhuman moral values. We know
that a man like Robespierre is the archetype of the
Puritan and the Lawgiver, a man of ascetic and utterly
sincere personal life, a man whose last appeal to the
French Convention was like his first:

A noble ideal based upon the scaffold; a dogma and a de-
tailed persecution side by side . . . to the last a strange mixture of lawyer and pedant and idealist. He would not act
without legal right, for his pedantry forbade it, nor move
with an armed minority, because, judged by his theories, it

would have been a crime. . . . He had the reserve, the dignity, the intense idealism, the perfect belief in himself, the certitude that others were in sympathy—all the characteristics, in fine, which distinguish the Absolutists and the great Reformers. In his iron code of theory we seem to hear the ghost of Calvin; in his reiterated morals and his perpetual application of them there is the occasional sharp reminiscence of Hildebrand. The famous cry, "I have loved justice and hated iniquity, therefore I die in exile," is not so far distant from " . . . *de mourir pour le peuple et d' en être abhorré.*" (. . . to die for the people and then to be hated by them.)[5]

Contrast the behavior of Robespierre with that of Danton. Danton was shrewd where Robespierre was moral; human where Robespierre was exact. When Robespierre's Jacobins gained the upper hand, Danton was urged to make one last stand, to fight back. Danton, on the grounds that he was tired of being a leader and wanted to become a man again, refused to fight because it would mean more blood. And "I would rather be guillotined than guillotine." Danton was ready to take personal guilt and personal responsibility; but the Rousseauan conceptions of the human condition of which Robespierre was such a sterile prophet, categorically denied the old theological hypothesis that since man is inherently evil he must take guilt and responsibility. Rousseau and the Romantics contended that the system makes the man, and that the system is always evil. Men are in themselves good, but so long as they are bound and re-

stricted both socially and economically by a bad system,
they must do evil. The system forces a man to steal bread
for his starving children, or to cheat his neighbor in order to survive.

The prophets of the Reformation had posited the basic
problem of democracy as freedom of the conscience;
Rousseau and the later Romantics saw the problem as
freedom of the heart; the latter-day Marxists demanded
freedom of the belly. " 'Feed men, and then ask of them
virtue!' That's what they'll write on their banner, which
they will raise against Thee!" says Dostoyevsky's Inquisitor to Jesus Christ in the prison in Seville. In the allegory from *The Brothers Karamazov,* the Grand Inquisitor chides Christ for offering man his freedom, for freedom makes man unutterably unhappy. Man, says the
Inquisitor, wants contentment and bread; he needs authority in order to be contented, and bread in order to
be virtuous. In our time, this allegory of power and freedom has been carried to a strange conclusion: the exponents of political and religious freedom find themselves
more and more opposed to the exponents of economic
freedom, and each side would contend that man cannot
have freedom without losing security. It is felt, also, that
men can have either freedom or security only up to a
limited and sharply defined degree (for there is famine
in the Soviet Union from time to time, and there are
political persecutions in America).

The fascists sought neither freedom nor security, but

rather, the escape from all rational objectives whatsoever.

> Fascism is a real insurrection—an insurrection of *feeling*—
> a mutiny of *men* against the conditions of the modern world.
> It is completely characteristic of this aspect of Fascism in its
> early stages, both in Italy and in Germany, that the move-
> ment should have grown to full strength without either log-
> ical theory behind it or cut-and-dried program in front of
> it. The men who built Fascism in Italy and Germany . . .
> leave theories to the intellectuals and programs to the dem-
> ocrats who have betrayed them with programs for a cen-
> tury. The Fascist acts, in fact, instinctively, and not theo-
> retically.[6]

The objective, the real world, had somehow become too
awful for these people to contemplate, or to live with.
The revolt against mechanization and depersonalization
became the revolt of the lout (as H. G. Wells put it)
against civilization. And the end result of the fascist in-
surrection of feeling was a gray unfeeling state in which
everyone would seem to be good and heroic and sexless
and supposedly awaiting impatiently the chance, not to
live in excellence, but to die in a burst of glory. In this
again, lies the terrible paradox of politics. The revolt of
feeling ended in the methodical and scientific employment of mass murder; in a somewhat similar fashion, a
little less than two hundred years before, the revolt of
men after bread and liberty resulted in the methodical
guillotine.

The Russian revolutionary, Victor Serge, after being expelled from the Communist party and imprisoned in 1928, wrote that "everything had changed. . . . Morality: from the austere, sometimes implacable honesty of heroic Bolshevism, we gradually advance to unspeakable deviousness and deceit. . . . *It here becomes apparent that moral criteria sometimes have greater value than judgments based on political and economic considerations.*"[7]

Again, we must go outside of politics in order to find a rationale for the democratic society. What the old revolutionary has learned from bitter experience, we may learn less bitterly. And the final rationale is a moral criterion. Ernest Wall, in an article on Simone Weil, calls this criterion "metapolitics."

> [Simone Weil] knows that the secret of social redemption does not lie in politics, not even in a church-dominated politics. . . . It was never right, she asserted, that, because of political ineptitude or social negligence, people should be oppressed by excessive fatigue, harassing money worries, lack of true culture, or should know want, strife, or violence. However, she is equally sure that the mere absence of these human limitations would not of themselves facilitate the perception, let alone the achievement, of the divine ideal for human personality. In theory, better wages, less working hours, lighter burdens, and national peace should give the opportunity and lead to the desire for true culture; but in experience, these things fail to bring to men the true welfare of the soul.[8]

In the end we find that the rationale for democracy, if it is well-founded, must be based on a progressive social ideal: "better wages, less working hours, lighter burdens, and national peace." But these things in themselves are not enough, anymore than the idea that democracy is a good way of life simply because it *works better* is enough. We cannot separate the democratic idea from the Christian concept of life; we cannot separate our desire for social progress and the entire Judeo-Christian ethic which lies behind our desire.

The democratic idea is, first of all, a reasonable one. There is nothing which so characterizes the totalitarian tyrannies of our time so much as their increasing unreasonableness, the terrifying totality of their rejection of the full human personality. Reasonableness—the use of reason—means working on the assumption that there exists a meaningful reality whose existence does not depend upon our knowledge of it. The world in which we live is a cosmos and not a chaos. And man is endowed with the faculty of reasoning, and therefore of grasping —however dimly—the meaning of this reality. Knowledge involves the discovery of what exists.

This reasonableness means, among other things, individual responsibility—individual responsibility in a larger sense than the buying of the groceries, the keeping of oneself alive, and the pursuit of one's own business. Highly indicative of how lightly this wider responsibility is taken is the fact that the atomic scientists who became

concerned about the terrible destructive possibilities of
the Bomb which they had wrought were told, in effect,
"Your moral squeamishness does not interest us. Scientists know nothing of politics. Politics is our job; the
Bomb is your job. The using of the Bomb is our business
and not yours." And this happened in a country where
for two hundred years or so the expressed ideal has been
to make every man a citizen—and in that sense, a politician—in his own right. To say to an American worker:
"You are a plumber, and therefore your ideas on what
society means and how men should live are of no importance to us because it is none of your business
(plumbing is your business)"—would, I think, still elicit
cries of protest from many of us. However, when the
atomic scientists were told this, no such universal cry
arose, because, for many Americans, the idea that scientists should "mind their own business" was a comforting
thought; scientists are intellectuals, after all, and everyone knows what a meddlesome high-falutin' lot intellectuals are.

> The dominant characteristic of the intellectual climate of our
> times, curiously enough, is an animus against everything in-
> tellectual. Never was the rationality of man subjected to a
> more sustained attack than it is today, and from all quar-
> ters, scientific, philosophical, and even theological. And this
> is a curious fact that we should be using the methods of
> science, philosophy, and theology to discredit the existence
> of the very thing upon which the validity of those methods

depends, namely, the rationality of man and of the universe he inhabits.[9]

But the democratic idea is not merely a rational one; it is also, and by definition, ethical. Only on an ethical level do the dichotomies between the individual and society become solvable.

"It is wrong," says Simone Weil, "to be an 'I.' It is worse to be a 'We.' " What she means is that there is a unity above the social, a "belonging" above the membership of any group. Our goal is a unity which is born of the consciousness of "the All"—the allness of humanity and the allness of God; it is a sense of being part of the universal Whole.[10]

Because we believe in a cosmos rather than a chaos, we believe in the power of reason to find the patterns in the cosmos, to describe those patterns. From this comes the democratic concept that men are capable of making their own choices, of governing themselves, of mastering their destinies. And this democratic concept relates back to the "radical freedom of the self" to make choices.

True freedom requires both knowledge of the good and the will to choose from the good when known. The denial of either is a denial of freedom, and the denial of freedom is the rejection of that moral agony in man which characterizes his humanity. In one of the best analyses of the rise of National Socialism in Germany, Helmut Kuhn explains the acceptance of Hitler as being made possible by a "flight from freedom into forgetfulness." *"Freedom,"* *he says, "is* *rational choice. . . . "* For better or for worse, as Kuhn has said, man "is an altogether unique being, projecting, as it were, into a dimension foreign to animality."[11]

The escape into forgetfulness is always an illusion. Man thirsts for righteousness; if he does not find the way to true righteousness, he will probably descend into self-righteousness, like Torquemada, like Robespierre. And in one sense, and in one sense only, whichever way the dice falls, we win.

> [Metapolitics] helps us to eliminate our anthropomorphic ideas which limit God to the point of making him vulnerable to the attacks of evil . . . though we fail, or political schemes and social plans fail, Truth is such, Good is such, God is such, that ultimate failure is impossible.[12]

Only if we hold these two bases for the democratic community in mind—reason and ethics—can we have an understanding of what the wider sense of this concept does mean. The democratic idea in its largest sense cannot be limited to a governmental form; the philosophy behind it is one of rational and ethical judgment. And if we are genuinely assured that the democratic concept is a good one, worth struggling to improve, we need not boast of our claim; we need never talk in such loud voices about the American way of life. Given the fact of genuine assurance, we could be almost as modest as E. M. Forster:

> Two cheers for democracy; one because it admits variety and two because it permits criticism. Two cheers are quite enough; there is no occasion to give three. Only Love, the Beloved Republic, deserves that. . . . [13]

The Affirmation[14]

The Brethren and Mennonite sects which nurtured me are known as Withdrawing Sects. Convinced that the world, as they knew it in the early seventeenth and through the first quarter of the eighteenth century, was evil, they determined to render unto Caesar only the minimum loyalty. As pacifists they renounced war and the national state system which caused war. Believing that the church when allied with the state becomes inevitably the servant of a worldly kingdom, these ancestors of mine stressed "no force in religion." At the very center of their witness was the Love Feast, and the washing of feet—the symbolic act of the suffering servant. In a word, theirs was a miniature, beloved Republic of Love.

Hounded out of Europe, these religious sectarians found refuge in America, and built their islands of *Freundschaft* and *Gemeinschaft* (Friendship and Community). These islands have not even in our own time been assimilated by the world.

My island is near Goshen, Indiana. To be exact, my island is in the Baugo congregation—a Brethren family church made up almost entirely of relatives. Grandfather Schwalm was elder of our church. He ruled it as he did his family, with a gentle and firm hand. With few exceptions, my cousins lived their lives as did their fathers before them, that is, as hard-working and prosperous farmers. To this day I often wonder why I left in order to live out a different kind of pilgrimage. Perhaps I left because of some realization that there are no islands anymore, not even Brethren and Mennonite islands.

But even though I left, I was, willy-nilly, inheritor of the curse of the Brethren (a curse certainly not confined to the Brethren but intensely emphasized among them). This curse is a sense of purpose, a thing which has been known to drive men mad. I have lived my life with the conviction that the "love" or Agape ethic of my fathers must be universalized. And today I believe that if it is not universalized, man faces genocide on a total scale. In the words of Toynbee, the world faces a choice between unity and death.

The impending nature of this choice ultimately took me away from Baugo. In 1914 the Archduke Franz Ferdinand was shot, and the chain of events was precipitated which brought profound shocks to our church and community. Our boys—my friends, uncles, or cousins— had to choose between the Army (Caesar) or the jails reserved for conscientious objectors. All but one at Baugo chose the latter. Our church was daubed with yellow paint because our parents refused to buy Liberty Bonds; German was dropped from my high school classes. Hamburger became Salisbury steak; sauerkraut was named Liberty Cabbage; and Uncle John Martin tried to preach my grandmother's funeral sermon in English. Germans became Huns and baby killers, and all my nearest and dearest were Germans who spoke the Pennsylvania Dutch dialect. I wondered why all the Germans I read about were so satanic, and all I knew so saintly. I finally rationalized this dilemma by deciding that all the good Germans came to the United States to become my ancestors, while all the bad Germans stayed behind. Meanwhile, war prosperity was our prosperity too.

The path leading out of these complex circumstances was long and painful. Today I believe that the educated man is he who can see all the consequences of his acts in the sum total of their relationships. The mature man is he who not only sees, but acts upon what he sees.

As I look back now upon the Baugo of my youth, I am convinced that living in that long-age face-to-face world made less demands on me than the complicated world of my maturity. It takes more courage to face the day-by-day compromises which organized living demands, than to face the simple and straightforward demands of my Grandfather Schwalm.

Today, I am a teacher. As a teacher, I have but one desire: to produce tough-minded and functioning idealists. I learned long ago that there is no reason that the angels of light should not be so effective as the angels of darkness. Since someone must make decisions, better that the decision makers should belong to the world of light rather than of darkness. The pious used to ask me: "What are you, as a Brethren minister, doing in the

Congress of Industrial Organizations?" And I would answer: "Not that I am so good, but that the others are so awful." I rejoice whenever I make a good man a convert to the rough and tumble of politics, for I respect the political in myself more than I do the reformer.

It is the reformer who asserts that the politician is the product of the mores of the society in which he functions. And quite often the politician is less corrupt than the society itself. The nature of man is political, among other things; politicians deserve respectability. The peace, I tell my uncompromising fellow Brethren, will not descend like a dove, but must be hammered out, compromise by patient compromise, decision by painful decision. Forget about the White House, I tell parents when they point their sons to the presidency; help your children to find the precinct. It would be a step toward a better world if teachers of government were willing to recognize caucus and primary, and if they were less disparaging of smoke-filled rooms.

He has faith in democracy who can continue battling for the fulfillment of his dream, even though harassed by the day-to-day, the small, the needling disappointments. It takes more courage to stay in and take the buffeting than to withdraw into the island of the like-minded.

He has faith in democracy who knows what he believes, gets a base in organization, and goes to work!

Appendix

Footnotes by Chapters

CHAPTER 1. THE COMMON DESTINY

1. John Dewey, *Experience and Education* (New York: The Macmillan Company, 1938). By permission of Dr. E. I. F. Williams, Heidelberg College, Tiffin, Ohio.

2. José Ortega y Gasset, *The Revolt of the Masses* (New York: W. W. Norton & Company, Inc., 1932), pp. 17-18. By permission of the publishers.

3. Erich, Fromm, *Man for Himself* (New York: Rinehart & Company, Inc., 1947), pp. 87, 71, 74. By permission of the publishers.

4. Jacques Maritain, *Education at the Crossroads* (New Haven: Yale University Press, 1943), pp. 20-22. By permission of the publishers.

5. *Ibid.*, pp. 34-35.

6. Erich, Fromm, *Man for Himself*, p. 19. By permission of Rinehart & Company, Inc.

7. Jacques Maritain, *Education at the Crossroads*, p. 15. By permission of the Yale University Press.

8. José Ortega y Gasset, *The Revolt of the Masses*, pp. 75, 77, 80. By permission of W. W. Norton & Company, Inc.

9. W. H. Auden, "Transplanted Englishman Views U. S.," Seventy-fifth Anniversary Supplement, *St. Louis Post-Dispatch*, Sunday, Dec. 13, 1953, p. 21. By permission of *St. Louis Post-Dispatch*.

10. W. H. Auden, *loc. cit.*

11. Bernard De Voto, Ed., *The Portable Mark Twain* (New York: The Viking Press, Inc., 1946). From Introduction by Bernard De Voto, p. 16. By permission of the publishers.

12. Graham Greene, *The Power and the Glory* (New York: The Viking Press, Inc., 1946).

13. C. Hartley Grattan, "James T. Farrell: Moralist," *Harper's Magazine*, Oct., 1954, p. 94.

14. Arthur Mizener, *The Far Side of Paradise* (Boston: Houghton Mifflin Company, 1949), p. 178. By permission of the publishers.

15. Henry Steele Commager, Ed., *Living Ideas in America* (New York: Harper & Brothers, 1951), p. 33. By permission of the publishers.

16. Henry Steele Commager, Ed., *Living Ideas in America*, pp. 33-34. By permission of Harper & Brothers.

17. An excellent documentation of the migrations to California is a book by Carey McWilliams entitled *Factories in the Field* (Boston: Little, Brown & Company, 1939).

18. Newton Edwards, "The Evolution of American Educational Ideals," Chapter 1 in *Education in a Democracy*, Newton Edwards, Ed. (Chicago: University of Chicago Press), pp. 6-7. By permission. Copyright 1941 by the University of Chicago.

19. W. Lloyd Warner, Robert J. Havighurst, and Martin B. Loeb. *Who Shall Be Educated?* (New York: Harper & Brothers, 1944), p. 57. By permission of the publishers.

20. Robert J. Havighurst, "Education for Social Cohesion in a Democracy," Chapter 2 in *Education in a Democracy*, Newton Edwards, Ed. (Chicago: University of Chicago Press), pp. 24-27. By permission. Copyright 1941 by the University of Chicago.

21. *Ibid.*, p. 38.

22. Alfred North Whitehead, *The Aims of Education* (New York: The Macmillan Company, New American Library edition, 1929), p. 52. By permission of the publishers.

23. Lee J. Cronbach, *Educational Psychology* (New York: Harcourt, Brace and Company, Inc., 1954), pp. 28-29. By permission of the publishers.

24. Gerhart Saenger, *The Social Psychology of Prejudice* (New York: Harper & Brothers, 1953), p. 192. By permission of the publishers.

25. *Ibid.*, pp. 193-194.

26. Mandel Sherman, "Education and the Process of Individual Adjustment," in *Education in a Democracy*, Newton Edwards, Ed. (Chicago: University of Chicago Press), pp. 68-69. By permission. Copyright 1941 by the University of Chicago.

27. Robert Redfield, *The Educational Experience*, published by the Fund for Adult Education, Pasadena, Calif., April, 1955. By permission of the author.

CHAPTER 2.   THE TIME-CLOCK HEART

1. *Automation*, A Report to the UAW-CIO Economic and Collective Bargaining Conference, held in Detroit, Mich., Nov. 12-13, 1954.

2. Francis W. Coker, Ed., *Democracy, Liberty, and Property* (New York: The Macmillan Company, 1942), adapted from pp. 236-237 of Chapter 23, written by Frederick Jackson Turner. By permission of the publishers.

3. Newton Edwards, Ed., *Education in a Democracy* (Chicago: University of Chicago Press), p. 8. By permission. Copyright 1941 by the University of Chicago.

4. *Automation*, CIO Committee on Economic Policy, Pamphlet 270.

5. Nat Weinberg, in *The Saturday Review*, Dec. 18, 1954. By permission of *The Saturday Review*.

6. Editorial in *Life* Magazine, January 17, 1955. By permission of the publishers.

7. George Orwell, *Dickens, Dali, and Others* (New York: Harcourt, Brace and Company, Inc., Doubleday edition, 1954), p. 127. By permission of the publishers.

8. Vincent Sheean, *Personal History* (New York: Random House, Inc., 1934), pp. 334-336. By permission of Curtis Brown, Ltd., agents for Mr. Sheean.

9. Lewis Mumford, *The Condition of Man* (New York: Harcourt, Brace and Company, Inc., 1944), pp. 167-168. By permission of the publishers.

10. Francis W. Coker, Ed., *Democracy, Liberty, and Property* (New York: The Macmillan Company, 1942), pp. 4-6. By permission of the publishers.

11. Lewis Mumford, *The Condition of Man*, p. 167. By permission of Harcourt, Brace and Company, Inc.

12. Werner Bloomburg, University of Chicago, "Mass Production, Automation and the Unmechanical Man," an unpublished article. By permission of the author.

13. Reinhold Niebuhr in *The Saturday Review*, Dec. 18, 1954. By permission of *The Saturday Review*.

CHAPTER 3. GOVERNMENT BY LAW AND GOVERNMENT BY MEN

1. Henri Beyle (Stendhal), *The Charterhouse of Parma* (New York: Liveright Publishing Corporation, Doubleday edition; Copyright, R, 1953, George Scott Moncrieff), p. 104, 114. By permission of Liveright Publishing Corporation.

2. In this more personally written section, "I Receive a Subpoena," Kermit Eby is speaking.

3. John Stuart Mill, *On Liberty* (Chicago: Henry Regnery Company, 1949), p. 32.

4. George Orwell, *Such, Such Were the Joys* (New York: Harcourt, Brace and Company, Inc., Doubleday edition, 1954), pp. 205-206. By permission of Harcourt, Brace and Company, Inc.

5. William Haller, *The Rise of Puritanism* (New York: Columbia University Press, 1938), p. 5. By permission of the publishers.

6. W. K. Jordan, *The Development of Religious Toleration in England, 1640-1660* (Cambridge: Harvard University Press, 1938), pp. 49-51. By permission of the publishers.

7. *Ibid.*, p. 10.

8. Will Durant, *The Renaissance* (New York: Simon and Schuster, Inc., 1953), p. 147. By permission of the publishers.

9. W. K. Jordan, *The Development of Religious Toleration in England, 1640-1660*, pp. 145-147. By permission of Harvard University Press.

10. *Ibid.*, p. 199.

11. *Ibid.*, p. 190.

12. Edward Dowden, *Puritan and Anglican* (London: Routledge & Kegan Paul, Ltd.), p. 211. By permission of the publishers.

13. Don M. Wolfe, Ed., *Milton and the Puritan Revolution* (New York: Thomas Nelson and Sons, 1941), p. 123, from Milton's *Defence*.

14. Walter Raleigh, Ed., *The Complete Works of the Marquess of Halifax* (New York: Oxford University Press, Inc., 1921), p. 129. By permission of the publishers.

15. Coffin and Witherspoon, *Seventeenth Century Prose and Poetry* (New York: Harcourt, Brace and Company, Inc., 1952), p. 704. By permission of the publishers.

16. John Stuart Mill, *On Liberty* (Chicago: Henry Regnery Company, 1949), p. 110.

17. From a speech given by Homer A. Jack, Ph.D., minister of the Unitarian Church, Evanston, Illinois, at the City Club of Chicago on May 10, 1954.

18. Figures taken from Documentary Report No. 1, *The Trumbull Park Homes Disturbance*, compiled by the Commission on Human Relations, 54 W. Hubbard St., Chicago, March, 1954.

19. Gerhart Saenger, *The Social Psychology of Prejudice* (New York: Harper & Brothers, 1953), p. 81. By permission of the publishers.

20. Alan Paton, "Negro in the North," *Collier's Magazine*, Oct. 29, 1954, pp. 72-75. By permission of the publishers and the author.

21. Homer A. Jack, from speech, "What Is Behind the Trumbull Park Disturbances?"

22. Alan Paton, "Negro in the North," Collier's Magazine, Oct. 29, 1954. By permission of the publishers and the author.

23. Robert Gruenberg, "Trumbull Park: Act II, The Elizabeth Wood Story," *The Nation*, Sept. 18, 1954. By permission of *The Nation*.

24. Gerhart Saenger, *The Social Psychology of Prejudice*, p. 10. By permission of Harper & Brothers.

25. *Ibid.*, p. 14.

26. Alan Paton, "Negro in the North," *Collier's Magazine*, Oct. 29, 1954, p. 75. By permission of the publishers and the author.

27. Alexander Herzen, in *My Past and Thoughts*, quoted from *The Romantic Exiles*, Edward Hallet Carr (London: Victor Gollanz, Ltd., 1933). Herzen was comparing midnineteenth century Czarist Russia with England.

28. Alan Paton, "Negro in the North," *Collier's Magazine*, Oct. 29, 1954, p. 74. By permission of the publishers and the author.

29. John Dewey, *Experience and Education* (New York: The Macmillan Company, 1938), pp. 57-59. By permission of Dr. E. I. F. Williams, Heidelberg College, Tiffin, Ohio.

30. Leo Strauss, *On Tyranny* (Glencoe, Ill.: The Free Press, 1948), pp. 55-60. By permission of the publishers.

31. W. J. Cash, *The Mind of the South* (New York: Doubleday and Company, Inc., 1941), pp. 55-56. By permission of Alfred A. Knopf, Inc., copyright owners.

32. Francis W. Coker, Ed., *Democracy, Liberty and Property* (New York: The Macmillan Company, 1942), p. 3. By permission of the publishers.

33. *Ibid.*, p. 10.

34. *Ibid.*, p. 10 also.

35. Max Radin, *The Law and You* (New York: New American Library of World Literature, 1948), p. 166.

36. Lewis Mumford, *The Condition of Man* (New York: Harcourt, Brace and Company, Inc., 1944), p. 192. By permission of the publishers.

37. José Ortega y Gasset, *The Revolt of the Masses* (New York: W. W. Norton & Co., Inc., 1932), p. 83. By permission of the publishers.

38. Murray Kempton, *Part of Our Time* (New York: Simon and Schuster, Inc., 1955), pp. 45-46. By permission of the publishers.

39. *Ibid.*, p. 49.

40. *Ibid.*, p. 49, also, quoting from *Boston* by Upton Sinclair.

41. Rita James, Law School, University of Chicago, "Negligence Awards and Social Status," an unpublished paper. By permission of the author.

42. An excellent example of a law created by and for a special interest group is, of course, the poll tax. M. R. Davie says that "the poll tax laws, most of them enacted between 1890 and 1910, were passed for two main reasons: first, to eliminate the Negro from politics after Reconstruction; second, to crush the radical agrarian movement which swept the West and parts of the South in the 1890's and 1900's. The Populist movement threatened for a time to unite the poor white and black masses against the ruling classes in the South. In Georgia and Alabama, where the Populist movement was very strong, the poll tax laws were the most severe. The application of this tax, which keeps about half of the whites and nearly all the Negroes from voting, marked the beginning of the Southern oligarchy that continues to hold sway in the seven poll-

tax states." (M. R. Davie, *Negroes in American Society* (New York: McGraw-Hill Book Company, Inc., 1949), p. 267. By permission of the publishers.

CHAPTER 4. GOVERNMENT BY MEN AND GOVERNMENT BY LOBBY

1. In this more personally written section, "The Teachers' Union," Kermit Eby is speaking.
2. Alexis De Tocqueville, *Democracy in America* (New York: Vintage Books, Inc., 1954), Vol. II, pp. 126-127. By permission of Alfred A. Knopf, Inc., copyright owners.
3. *Ibid.*, p. 124.
4. Henry Adams, *The Education of Henry Adams* (Boston: Houghton Mifflin Company, 1918). By permission of the publishers.
5. *Report of 1953 United Auto Workers' Convention,* pp. 51-55.
6. From "Historic New Contracts," *Ammunition,* June, 1955, p. 5.
7. Niccolo Machiavelli, *The Prince* (Chicago: Henry Regnery Company, 1948), pp. 62-63.
8. *Ibid.*, pp. 64-65.
9. Karl Schriftgiesser, *The Lobbyists* (Boston: Little, Brown & Company, 1951), pp. 5-6. By permission of the publishers.
10. Ray Allen Billington, *The United States: American Democracy in World Perspective: 1492-1947* (New York: Rinehart & Co., Inc., 1947), p. 253.
11. Karl Schriftgiesser, *The Lobbyists,* p. 47. By permission of Little, Brown & Company.
12. *Ibid.*, p. 51, quoting Marcus Duffield in *King Legion.*
13. Vernon Louis Parrington, *Main Currents in American Thought* (New York: Harcourt, Brace and Company, Inc., 1930), pp. 3-4. By permission of the publishers.
14. Henry Adams, *The Education of Henry Adams* (Boston: Houghton Mifflin Company, 1918), p. 424. By permission of the publishers.
15. *Ibid.*, p. 335.
16. *Ibid.*, p. 225.
17. *Ibid.*, p. 33.
18. *Ibid.*, p. 421.
19. Francis W. Coker, Ed., *Democracy, Liberty and Property* (New York: The Macmillan Company, 1942), pp. 388-389. By permission of the publishers.

CHAPTER 5. A STANDARD TO WHICH THE JUST CAN REPAIR

1. Thomas Hobbes, *Leviathan* (Chicago: Henry Regnery Company, 1949), p. 77.
2. *Ibid.*, p. 72.
3. *The Dialogues of Plato*, trsl. by B. Jowett (New York: Random House, Inc., 1937), Vol. I, pp. 414-415. By permission of Oxford University Press, Inc., copyright owners.
4. John Stuart Mill, *On Liberty* (Chicago: Henry Regnery Company, 1949), p. 32.
5. Hilaire Belloc, *Danton* (London: James Nisbet and Co., Ltd., 1899), pp. 306, 285, 312. By permission of the publishers.
6. James Drennan, B.U.F., *Oswald Mosely and British Fascism* (London: J. Murray, 1934), pp. 212-213.
7. Victor Lvovich Kibalchich (Victor Serge), *From Lenin to Stalin* (New York: Pioneer Publications, Inc., 1937).
8. Ernest Wall, "Simone Weil and Metapolitics," *Religion in Life*, Summer, 1955, Vol. XXIV, No. 3, p. 421. By permission of *Religion in Life* and the author.
9. John H. Hallowell, *The Moral Foundation of Democracy* (Chicago: University of Chicago Press), p. 23. By permission. Copyright 1954 by the University of Chicago.
10. Ernest Wall, "Simone Weil and Metapolitics," *Religion in Life*, Summer, 1955, Vol. XXIV, No. 3. By permission of *Religion in Life* and the author.
11. John H. Hallowell, *The Moral Foundation of Democracy* (Chicago: University of Chicago Press), pp. 112, 104. By permission. Copyright 1954 by the University of Chicago.
12. Ernest Wall, *loc. cit.*, p. 423.
13. E. M. Forster, *What I Believe* (London: The Hogarth Press, Ltd., 1939), p. 19.
14. In this more personally written section, "The Affirmation," Kermit Eby is again speaking.

HADDAM HOUSE BOOKS